PRETTY PARTY CAKES

PRETTY PARTY CAKES

sweet and stylish cakes and cookies for all occasions

PEGGY PORSCHEN

PHOTOGRAPHY BY GEORGIA GLYNN SMITH

CLARKSON POTTER/PUBLISHERS
NEW YORK

I dedicate this book to my parents, Iris and Helmut,
for giving me support and encouragement
in everything I always wanted to do.

Editorial Director: Jane O'Shea
Creative Director: Helen Lewis
Editor and Project Manager: Lewis Esson
Photography: Georgia Glynn Smith
Designer: Chalkley Calderwood Pratt

Published in the United States by Clarkson Potter/Publishers, an imprint
of the Crown Publishing Group, a division of Random House, Inc., New York.
www.crownpublishing.com
www.clarksonpotter.com

Originally published in Great Britain by Quadrille Publishing Limited,
London, in 2005.

Library of Congress Cataloging-in-Publication Data is available upon
request.

ISBN-13: 978-0-307-33603-3
ISBN-10: 0-307-33707-3

Printed in China

Reprinted in 2006, 2007 (twice), 2008
10 9 8 7 6 5

First American Edition

contents

basics

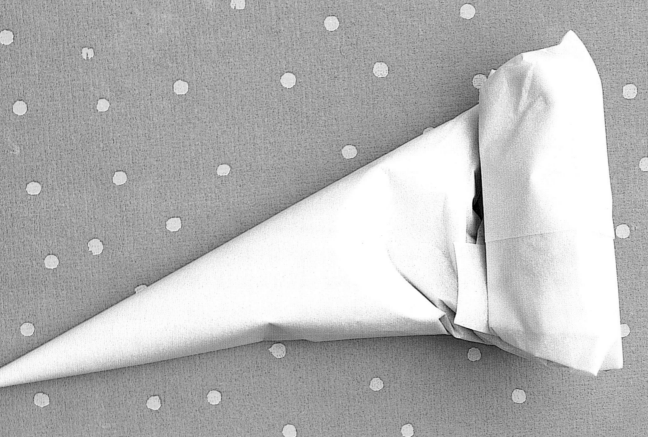

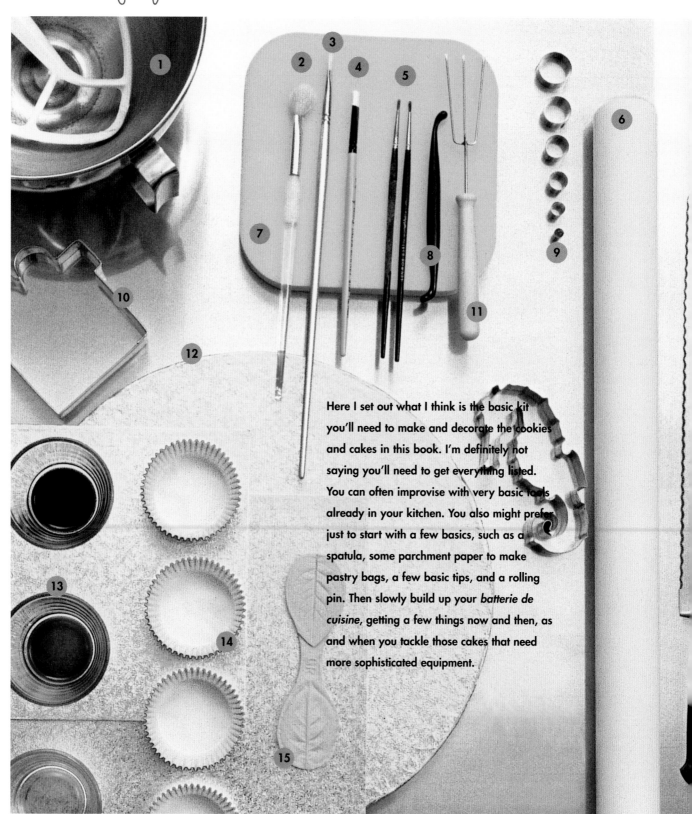

Here I set out what I think is the basic kit you'll need to make and decorate the cookies and cakes in this book. I'm definitely not saying you'll need to get everything listed. You can often improvise with very basic tools already in your kitchen. You also might prefer just to start with a few basics, such as a spatula, some parchment paper to make pastry bags, a few basic tips, and a rolling pin. Then slowly build up your *batterie de cuisine*, getting a few things now and then, as and when you tackle those cakes that need more sophisticated equipment.

1 Kitchen Aid mixer (metal bowl with paddle attachment)

2-5 decorating brushes (preferably at least 2)

6 large rolling pin

7 foam pad (see page 142)

8 dog tool (see page 142)

9 assorted round cutters

10 various shaped cookie cutters

11 chocolate dipping fork

12 cake boards in various shapes and sizes

13 range of food colors

14 paper baking cases

15 leaf veiner (see page 142)

16 metal side scraper

17 flower nail (see page 142)

18 paper pastry bags

19 edible glitter in several colors

20 daisy cutter (see page 142)

21 small plastic board

22 large serrated knife

23-4 large and small spatulas

25 lollipop sticks

26 small rolling pin

* range of cookie sheets

* selection of bowls

* wire cooling rack

* baking pans for large cakes

* muffin tray

* large angled spatula (see page 142)

* parchment and waxed papers

* cellophane and plastic wrap

* cardboard

* pencils

* strong scissors

* small needle

* turntable (optional but useful)

* pastry brush

* fondant smoothers

* rose calyx cutter (see page 142)

* rose leaf cutter (see page 142)

* ¼-inch guide sticks

* plastic dowels

* edible shimmer dust in several colors

baking basic cookies ℓℓ

Always bake equally sized cookies together to make sure they bake in the same time. If you mix different sizes, the smaller ones are baked when the larger ones are still raw in the middle.

BASIC SUGAR COOKIES

MAKES ABOUT 30 COOKIES

1¾ sticks unsalted soft butter

1 cup sugar

1 extra-large egg, lightly beaten

3 cups all-purpose flour, plus more
    for dusting

OPTIONAL FLAVORS:

for vanilla cookies, add seeds from
    1 vanilla bean

for lemon cookies, add finely grated
    zest of 1 lemon

for orange cookies, add finely grated
    zest of 1 orange

for chocolate cookies, replace scant
    ½ cup of the all-purpose flour with

scant ½ cup unsweetened cocoa
powder

EQUIPMENT

✳ **Kitchen Aid or electric mixer with**
    paddle attachment

✳ **plastic wrap**

✳ **¼-inch guide sticks**

✳ **large rolling pin**

✳ **cookie cutters in various shapes**

✳ **small spatula**

✳ **cookie sheet**

✳ **parchment or waxed paper**

✳ **wire cooling rack**

1 In a Kitchen Aid or electric mixer with paddle attachment, cream the butter with the sugar and chosen flavoring until well mixed and just creamy in texture. Do not overwork, or the cookies will spread during baking.

2 Beat in the egg until well combined. Add the flour and mix on low speed until a dough forms (see 1). Gather into a ball, wrap in plastic wrap and chill for at least 1 hour.

3 Place the dough on a floured surface and knead briefly. Using two ¼-inch guide sticks, roll out to an even thickness (see 2).

4 Use cookie cutters to cut out shapes (see 3) and, using a spatula, lay on a cookie sheet lined with parchment or waxed paper. Chill again for about 30 minutes. Preheat the oven to 350°F.

5 Bake for 8 to 12 minutes, depending on size, until golden brown at the edges. Let cool on a wire rack.

GINGERBREAD COOKIES

MAKES ABOUT 30 COOKIES

1¾ sticks unsalted butter, diced

1 teaspoon baking soda

3⅔ cups all-purpose flour

FOR THE HOT MIX:

¾ cup packed dark brown sugar

6 tablespoons honey

2 tablespoons orange juice

2 tablespoons ground cinnamon

2 tablespoons ground ginger

1 teaspoon allspice

seeds from 1 vanilla bean

pinch of salt

EQUIPMENT

* deep heavy-bottom saucepan
* wooden spoon
* Kitchen Aid or electric mixer with paddle attachment
* sifter
* plastic wrap
* large rolling pin
* ¼-inch guide sticks
* assorted cookie cutters
* small spatula
* cookie sheet
* parchment or waxed paper
* wire cooling rack

1 Place all the ingredients for the hot mix in a deep heavy-bottom saucepan and bring to a boil, stirring from time to time (see 1).

2 Remove the pan from the heat and, using a wooden spoon, carefully stir in the butter (see 2).

3 Once well combined, add the baking soda and whisk the mixture through briefly.

4 Pour into the bowl of a Kitchen Aid or electric mixer and leave to cool until it is just slightly warm.

5 Sift the flour over the mixture and combine on low speed, using the paddle until a dough forms (see 3).

6 Wrap the dough in plastic wrap and chill for a couple of hours or overnight.

7 Place the dough on a floured clean surface and knead it briefly. Then roll it between two ¼-inch guide sticks to an even thickness.

8 Use cookie cutters to cut out shapes and, using a spatula, lay these on a cookie sheet lined with parchment or waxed paper.

9 Chill again for about 30 minutes. Preheat the oven to 400°F.

10 Bake the cookies for 10 minutes until just firm to the touch.

11 Lift the cookies off the tray and leave to cool on a wire rack. Wrapped in foil or plastic wrap, these will keep well in a cool dry place for up to a month. (The basic sugar cookies opposite will also keep this way.)

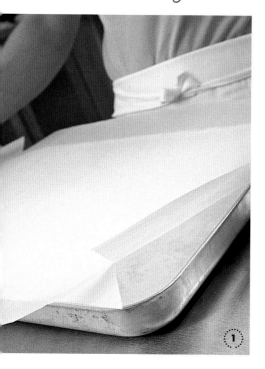
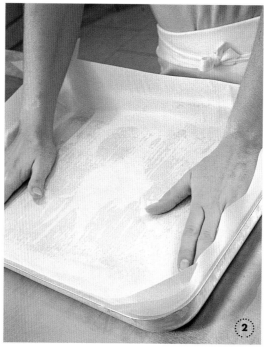

For the best tasting basic cake, you really need to insure you only use the best quality ingredients—butter, flour, eggs, and sugar, as well as flavorings—even if they are a bit more expensive. Personally, I am a big fan of organic products and free-range eggs.

BASIC SHEET CAKE

MAKES ONE 12 X 16-INCH CAKE, OR THREE 8-INCH CAKES, OR ABOUT 50 CUPCAKES

3½ sticks salted butter, softened

2 cups sugar

8 large eggs, at room temperature

3 cups self-rising flour

a little vegetable oil

OPTIONAL FLAVORS:

for a vanilla cake, add seeds from 2 vanilla beans

for a lemon cake, add finely grated zest of 4 lemons

for an orange cake, add finely grated zest of 4 oranges

for a chocolate cake, replace scant 1 cup of the self-rising flour with scant 1 cup of unsweetened cocoa powder and add 3½ ounces melted dark Belgian chocolate to the butter and sugar mix

EQUIPMENT

✳ Kitchen Aid or electric mixer with paddle attachment

✳ bowl

✳ baking pans for large cakes

✳ baking tray for fondant fancies

✳ muffin tray and paper cases for cupcakes

✳ parchment or waxed paper

✳ large spatula, small spoon, or large paper pastry bag (see page 25)

✳ wire cooling rack

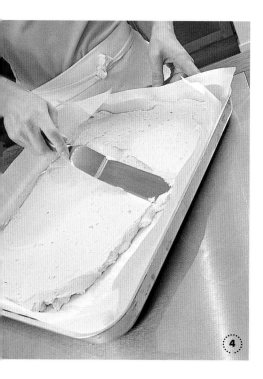

(4)

1 Preheat the oven to 400°F.

2 Place the butter, sugar, and chosen flavoring in the bowl of an electric mixer and, using the paddle attachment, cream together until pale and fluffy.

3 Beat the eggs lightly in another bowl and slowly add to the mix, while paddling on medium speed. If the mixture starts curdling, add a little bit of flour.

4 Once the eggs and the butter mixture are combined, mix in the flour at low speed.

5 For fondant fancies or large cakes, grease a baking tray or pan with a little vegetable oil. Cut a piece of parchment paper to fit

inside so it goes up the sides and is slightly higher than the sides all around (see 1), just in case the cake rises higher than them. Snip into the 4 corners so it will sit neatly (see 2). Fill evenly with the batter, using a large spatula (see 4).

6 For cupcakes, place the paper cases in the muffin tray and fill with the cake batter only up to half of their height. You can either use a small spoon or pipe the mix into the paper cases with the help of a large paper decorating bag.

7 Bake a large tray or pan for about 25 minutes, and cupcakes for only 12 to 15 minutes. Test the cake with a thin knife; it should come out clean when the cake is baked through.

8 Lift off the tray and leave the cake to cool on a wire rack. Wrap in plastic wrap to keep for up to a day in a cool, dry place. If you need to keep for longer, then wrap and chill for up to a week, or freeze.

MY FAVORITE CAKE AND FILLING COMBINATIONS

My cake recipes are very easy to make, but it is important that even the simplest cake is bursting with flavor. Below are some suggestions of my favorite combinations to guarantee this.

When flavoring sugar syrups and buttercreams, always do this the day before and leave them to infuse overnight, as the flavor will

then develop even more strongly.

It is important that a cake is well soaked with sugar syrup, as this gives it moisture and lots of flavor.

FOR VANILLA AND RASPBERRY CAKE USE:

✳ Vanilla cake
✳ Vanilla sugar syrup (see page 15) for soaking
✳ Vanilla buttercream (see page 14) and raspberry jam for layering

FOR LEMON AND LIMONCELLO CAKE USE:

✳ Lemon cake
✳ Sugar syrup (see page 15) flavored with lemon zest and Limoncello liqueur for soaking
✳ Lemon curd (I buy a good quality brand) and lemon-flavored buttercream (see page 14) for layering

FOR ORANGE AND GRAND MARNIER CAKE USE:

✳ Orange cake
✳ Sugar syrup (see page 15) flavored with orange zest and Grand Marnier for soaking
✳ Luxury orange marmalade (again from the supermarket) and orange-flavored buttercream (see page 14) for layering

FOR CHOCOLATE AND PEPPERMINT CAKE USE:

✳ Chocolate cake
✳ Sugar syrup (see page 15)
✳ Belgian chocolate ganache (see page 15) flavored with peppermint liqueur for layering

basic cake fillings ccccccccccccccccccccccccccccccccccccccccccc

The syrups and fillings I give here have proven to be among my most popular. You can, though, use whatever you like that tastes good, and make endless changes on these basic tastes.

BUTTERCREAM FROSTING

MAKES ABOUT 2¼ CUPS

2¼ sticks soft unsalted butter

generous 2 cups confectioners'
  sugar, sifted

OPTIONAL FLAVORS:

seeds from a vanilla bean

finely grated lemon zest

finely grated orange zest

EQUIPMENT

✻ Kitchen Aid or electric mixer with
  paddle attachment

1 Place the butter, sugar, and flavoring in the mixer bowl (see 1), and beat on medium speed until light and fluffy (see 2).

2 If not using immediately, store in a sealed container in the refrigerator and bring back to room temperature before use.

SUGAR SYRUP

MAKES ABOUT 2½ CUPS

1¼ cups sugar

OPTIONAL FLAVORS:

seeds from a vanilla bean

finely grated lemon zest and
   Limoncello liqueur

finely grated orange zest and
   Grand Marnier liqueur

peppermint liqueur

EQUIPMENT

✳ saucepan

✳ spoon

1 Place the sugar and 1 cup of
water in a saucepan, stir well and
bring to a boil; leave to cool down.

2 When lukewarm, add the
flavorings. Store in the refrigerator
if not using immediately.

BELGIAN CHOCOLATE GANACHE

MAKES ABOUT 2 CUPS

9 ounces light cream

9 ounces dark couverture chocolate
   chips (I use 55% cocoa—any
   darker and it splits more readily)

OPTIONAL FLAVORS:

orange or peppermint liqueur, or any
   other liqueur

EQUIPMENT

✳ saucepan

✳ bowl

✳ whisk

1 Place the cream in a saucepan
and bring to a boil.

2 Place the chocolate in a bowl.
Pour the cream over (see 1) and
stir together using a whisk (see 2).

3 Let cool slightly, until just
beginning to harden (see 3),
before use.

4 If not using immediately,
store in a sealed container in the
refrigerator and bring back to
room temperature before use.

filling and covering large cakes ℓℓℓℓℓℓℓℓℓℓℓℓℓℓℓℓℓℓℓℓℓℓℓ

The following instructions for various standard procedures cover all aspects of filling and assembling large and tiered cakes. Although the cake used here is square, the basic techniques demonstrated work equally well with round cakes, or any other shape.

MAKING A SQUARE TWO-TIERED CAKE

10-INCH AND 7-INCH

You'll need this exact procedure for making the Dropping Daisies cake on page 135, for example.

2 10-inch square cakes (1 recipe quantity of basic sheet cake batter, see page 12)

2 7-inch square cakes (½ recipe quantity of basic sheet cake batter, see page 12)

1¼ cups sugar syrup (see page 15), flavored to your choice

3⅓ cups buttercream (see page 14), flavored to your choice

plus a filling of your choice such as lemon curd or orange marmalade

EQUIPMENT

＊ **bread knife**
＊ **10-inch and 7-inch thin square cake boards**
＊ **pastry brush**
＊ **large spatula**
＊ **turntable**
＊ **side scraper**
＊ **2 trays, large enough for the cakes and able to fit in your refrigerator**

1 Using a bread knife, trim the top crust off the two larger cakes.

2 Place one of the cakes on a 10-inch cake board with a dab of buttercream to make it stick.

3 Using a pastry brush, soak the top of this layer well with the sugar syrup and then spread it with a thin layer of buttercream.

4 Soak the second cake with sugar syrup as well, then spread this with the chosen filling.

5 Turn this cake upside down and place it on the first cake so the buttercream and filling come together.

6 Soak the top of the sandwiched cake with sugar syrup.

7 Place the entire cake on top of the turntable and coat the outside of the cake with buttercream (see 1), spreading it first over the top, then down along the sides.

8 Use the spatula to level the top and a side scraper to straighten the sides (see 2).

9 Repeat the buttercream coating until you are happy with the shape. The cake should be level and straight for best results.

10 Repeat this entire process with the 7-inch cake. Chill both cakes for at least 1 hour, until the buttercream has set firmly.

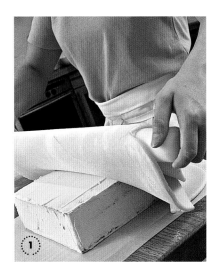

COVERING A CAKE WITH MARZIPAN AND ROLLED FONDANT

confectioners' sugar for dusting

5½ pounds white marzipan

a little buttercream (see page 14)

5½ pounds white ready-to-use rolled
 fondant

food color (here mint green)

alcohol or water, for brushing

EQUIPMENT

✳ large rolling pin

✳ ¼-inch guide sticks

✳ parchment or waxed paper

✳ large spatula

✳ small kitchen knife

✳ fondant smoothers

✳ pastry brush

✳ paper pastry bag (see page 25)

1 Start at least 2 days ahead. Place the cake on parchment or waxed paper. Thinly coat with buttercream to help the marzipan stick.

2 First work on the 10-inch tier: dust the counter top with confectioners' sugar, put 3⅓ pounds of marzipan on it and, with a rolling pin and ¼-inch guide sticks, roll to an even thickness large enough to cover the tier.

3 Using the rolling pin, lift the marzipan and lay it over the cake (see 1). Push it down the sides with your hand and insure there are no air pockets.

4 Trim excess marzipan off the sides with a kitchen knife (see 2).

5 Run the fondant smoothers along the sides and over the top of the cake until they all look nice and straight (see 3).

6 Repeat this complete process for the 7-inch tier, using the remaining marzipan.

7 Let the marzipan set for 1 to 2 days at a cool room temperature.

8 When the marzipan is firmly set, knead all the rolled fondant with some suitable food color until it has an even hue.

9 Brush a thin layer of alcohol or water over the larger marzipan-covered cake.

10 On a surface dusted with confectioners' sugar, roll out 3⅓ pounds of the fondant between ¼-inch guide sticks. Use to cover the cake following the same procedure as for applying the marzipan.

11 Repeat this process for the smaller cake, using the remaining fondant. Let the rolled fondant set for 1 or 2 days at room temperature.

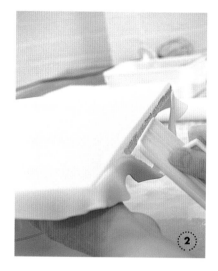

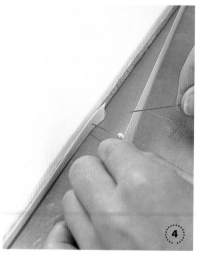

1 Dust the cake board thinly with confectioners' sugar and brush it with a little water. (This will make a glue for the rolled fondant.)

2 Roll the rolled fondant out to about ⅛ inch thick and large enough to cover the cake board.

3 Using the rolling pin, lift the fondant (see 1) and lay it over the cake board.

4 Let the fondant smoothers glide carefully over the surface of the fondant and push out any trapped air bubbles.

5 Place the board on top of the turntable, if using one, and push the rolled fondant down the sides with the fondant smoothers (see 2).

6 Trim the excess fondant off with a spatula (see 3) and let the fondant dry for 1 or 2 days.

7 Once the fondant is dry, wind the ribbon around the edge of the board and fix the ends with a metal pin (see 4).

COVERING A CAKE BOARD WITH ROLLED FONDANT

confectioners' sugar for dusting

9 ounces colored ready-to-use rolled fondant

EQUIPMENT

* 14-inch square cake board
* pastry brush
* rolling pin
* fondant smoothers
* turntable (optional)
* spatula
* 2½ yards white ribbon, ½ inch wide
* metal pin

TIERED CAKES

⅔ cup soft-peak royal icing (see page 24)

food color of choice (here mint green)

EQUIPMENT

✳ 14-inch iced cake board (see
  opposite)

✳ paper pastry bags (see page 25)

✳ large angled spatula

✳ 5-inch square template

✳ small needle

✳ 4 plastic dowels

✳ pencil

✳ strong scissors or serrated knife

1 Pipe some icing in the middle of the board to help secure the cake. Using the angled spatula, lift the larger tier (pages 16–17) and place in the middle of the board (see 1).

2 Place a 5-inch square template in the middle of the top of the lower tier and mark each corner with a needle (see 2).

3 Push a dowel into the cake at each mark (see 3). These will stop the top tier from sinking into the bottom. Mark with a pencil where they come out of the cake.

4 Lift out the dowels and, using strong scissors or a serrated knife, trim them ½ inch above the mark, then stick them back into the cake.

5 Pipe some royal icing into the middle of the bottom tier to secure the top tier in place and center the top tier on the bottom one.

6 Mix some icing with food color to match the rolled fondant and pipe a thin line along the bottom edge of each tier. While wet, run a finger over them to smooth (see 4).

Made from sugar, water, and cream of tartar, fondant is widely used in confectionery as well as in cake decorating. To keep it simple, I use ready-made fondant, which is available from specialist suppliers or (in a powdered version) from some supermarkets. Tightly wrapped in plastic wrap, it will keep for up to three months. It is important not to let the fondant boil at any time.

FONDANT ICING

MAKES ENOUGH FOR ABOUT 30 CUPAKES OR 50 FONDANT FANCIES

3⅓ pounds ready-made fondant

⅔ cup sugar syrup (see page 15)

1 tablespoon lemon juice

1 tablespoon glucose

selection of food colors

EQUIPMENT

✳ large microwave-proof bowl

✳ microwave

✳ large wooden or plastic spoon

1 Unless freshly made, place the fondant in a large microwave-proof bowl, cover with hot water and leave to soften for 15 minutes.

2 Pour away the water and add the remaining ingredients.

4 tablespoons sugar syrup (see page 15)**, flavored as you like**

FOR 12 FONDANT ICED CUPCAKES:

⅓ cup apricot jam, strained

1¾ cups fondant icing and food color of choice

FOR 12 CHOCOLATE CUPCAKES:

1¾ cups chocolate ganache (see page 15)

FOR 12 BUTTERCREAM CUPCAKES:

1⅓ cups buttercream (see page 14)

EQUIPMENT

❋ pastry brush

❋ saucepan

❋ small bowl

❋ small spatula or spoon

1 Using a pastry brush, soak the top of each of the cupcakes with sugar syrup.

2 For fondant-covered cupcakes, boil the strained apricot jam with a little water in a pan and brush it over each cup cake; let them dry.

3 Have your fondant icing ready in a small bowl and dip the top of each cupcake into the icing (see above).

4 Let the icing set and repeat the dipping process again for an even coating.

5 For chocolate or buttercream cupcakes, simply spread the topping over each cake using a small spatula or spoon.

3 Heat in the microwave for about 3 minutes at medium power. Stir to combine well, then heat for another minute.

4 For dipping cupcakes and fondant fancies, divide the fondant between small bowls and color each with different food colors, adding them a little drop at a time.

5 Before you start dipping, heat each bowl in the microwave for 10 to 20 seconds at full heat.

You want the fondant to be very warm (not boiling) to the touch.

6 Check the consistency of the fondant. If it feels thick and heavy when dipping, add a little more sugar syrup to thin it down until it runs smoothly.

CUPCAKES

FOR 12 CUPCAKES:

12 cupcakes (see Basic Sheet Cake, page 12)

FONDANT FANCIES

Using the fondant icing as shown on the previous pages, we can now make basic little fondant fancies. During my time working for Konditor & Cook, I must have produced literally thousands of such little fondant cakes—an experience that undoubtedly influenced my style. I now like to use lots of glitter and edible dust on them, as you can see in my fondant Heart Fancies on pages 70–1 and my signature Bollywood Kitsch Cakes on pages 66–7, etc.

FOR ABOUT 35

1 rectangular vanilla sheet cake
 (see page 12)

⅔ cup vanilla-flavored sugar syrup
 (see page 14)

½ cup vanilla buttercream
 (see page 15)

scant ½ cup seedless raspberry jam

2 ¼ pounds fondant icing (see page 20-1)

selection of food colors

⅔ cup apricot jam, strained

1 cup confectioners' sugar

18 ounces marzipan

EQUIPMENT

✳ bread knife

✳ tray

✳ plastic wrap

✳ small bowls

✳ pastry brush

✳ large rolling pin

✳ heart-shaped cutter, if required

✳ microwave

✳ chocolate dipping fork

✳ wire cooling rack

✳ paper baking cases

1 Using the bread knife, trim off the dark top layer from your cake and then turn it upside down on a tray.

2 Cut the cake horizontally in half. Set the top half aside.

3 Using a pastry brush, soak the top surface of the bottom cake with the vanilla syrup and spread it with the buttercream and then the raspberry jam. Sandwich with the top half of the cake. Wrap in plastic wrap and chill for at least 2 hours.

4 While it chills, prepare the icing: divide it among small bowls and mix with different food colors of your choice. Cover each bowl with plastic wrap and set aside.

5 Once the cake is cool and firm, warm up the apricot jam, unwrap the cake and, using the pastry brush, spread a thin layer of jam over the top.

6 Dust your counter top with confectioners' sugar and roll the marzipan out to a thickness of ⅛ inch. Cut it to the same size as the cake, lift it with a rolling pin and lay it on top of the cake (see 1).

7 Slice the marzipan-topped cake into 2-inch squares (see 2), or use the cutter to cut out heart shapes.

8 Brush the top of each piece with more apricot glaze.

9 Heat a bowlful of colored fondant in the microwave on medium heat for 20 seconds at a time, until it is warm and runny. (Alternatively, heat it in a heavy pan over very low heat, stirring constantly, if you don't have a microwave.) Do not let the fondant boil, or it will lose its shine.

10 Give the fondant a quick stir and start dipping your little cakes in it. First dip the cake into the fondant upside-down. To lift it out, hold it with one finger at the bottom of the cake and with a chocolate dipping fork at the top (see 3). Make sure you don't push the fork into the marzipan, just lift the cake gently and place it straight on to the wire cooling rack (see 4), then leave it for the icing to set.

11 Carefully remove the cakes from the rack and place in paper cases. This is best done with slightly wet fingers, to prevent the icing sticking to them.

STIFF-PEAK CONSISTENCY   SOFT-PEAK CONSISTENCY   RUNNY CONSISTENCY

Making and using royal icing is easier than you might think, but you can always buy a ready-to-mix version from a supermarket. This recipe makes a lot, but these quantities are easier to mix.

ROYAL ICING

MAKES ABOUT 2½ POUNDS

2 tablespoons eggwhite powder

2¼ pounds confectioners' sugar, sifted

1 tablespoon lemon juice

EQUIPMENT

✳ strainer

✳ Kitchen Aid or electric mixer with
   paddle attachment

✳ spoon

✳ sealable plastic container

✳ kitchen cloth

1 Mix the eggwhite powder with ⅔ cup of water and pass through a strainer to get rid of any lumps.

2 Place the sugar in the clean bowl of an electric mixer, add about three-quarters of the eggwhite mixture and the lemon juice, and start mixing on low speed.

3 Once the sugar and the eggwhite mixture are well combined, check the consistency. If the sides of the bowl still look dry and crumbly, add some more eggwhite mixture until the icing looks almost smooth, but not wet.

4 Keep mixing for about 4 to 5 minutes, until it reaches stiff-peak consistency.

5 Spoon into a plastic container, cover with a clean damp cloth and the lid; store at room temperature.

ROYAL ICING CONSISTENCIES

Throughout the book, I will refer to three useful consistencies of royal icing, which are important in achieving the right results. Simply thin down your basic royal icing with water, a little bit at a time, mixing with a spatula, until you have the right consistency. Keep your icing covered with plastic wrap or a damp cloth when not using it, to stop it from drying out.

STIFF-PEAK CONSISTENCY
for piping sugar flowers and leaves

SOFT-PEAK CONSISTENCY
for piping lines, dots and borders

RUNNY CONSISTENCY
for filling in the middle of spaces

MAKING A PASTRY BAG

1 Take a square of parchment or waxed paper about 14 x 14 inches and fold a corner over to the opposite corner. Cut through the fold with a sharp knife (see 1).

2 Take one of the resulting paper triangles and hold it with your left hand at the middle of the longest side and with your right hand at the corner on the opposite (see 2). Move your right hand over to the right corner and curl it over to the top corner, so it forms a cone (see 3).

3 Now move your left hand to the left corner and roll it around the cone until all corners meet at the top back of the cone. Adjust by moving them back and forth between your thumb and fingers until the cone forms a sharp point (see 4).

4 Now fold the corners over to the inside of the cone, tear it at each side of the seam and fold the flap inside. This insures the cone stays in shape without opening up (see 5).

5 To fill the bag, hold it in one hand and use a small spatula to fill it with the icing using the other

hand. Don't fill it more than half full, or the icing will squeeze out through the top when piping.

6 Close by folding the side with the seam over to the plain side twice.

BASIC PIPING TECHNIQUES

First snip a small tip off your piping bag already filled with icing.

PIPING LINES:

1 Hold the bag between thumb and fingers of your preferred hand and use the index finger of your other hand to guide the tip.

2 Touch the starting point with the tip of the bag and slowly squeeze out icing. As you squeeze, lift the bag slightly and pull the line straight toward you.

3 As you approach the finishing point, gradually bring the bag down, stop squeezing and drop the line by touching the finishing point.

PIPING DOTS:

1 Holding the tip just above the surface, squeeze the bag to produce a dot. Gradually lift the tip as the dot gets larger.

2 Once the dot is its desired size, stop squeezing and lift off the tip.

3 If the dot forms a little peak at the top, flatten it carefully with a damp soft decorating brush.

PIPING DOTTED BORDERS:

1 Start as for piping a dot. Once the dot has reached the required size, stop squeezing and pull the tip of your bag down, stopping where the next dot should start.

2 Repeat, making sure the dots are all the same size and equidistant. After a short while, you will get into a flowing motion and your border will look nice and even.

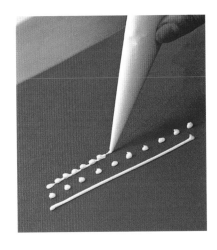

DAFFODILS

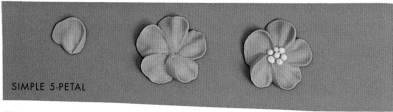

SIMPLE 5-PETAL

PANSIES

DAISIES

ROYAL ICED FLOWERS

Remember that for the piping of almost all flower shapes, you will want to use icing with a stiff-peak consistency.

EQUIPMENT

✻ metal piping tips for petal piping (for example Wilton 104, PME 56R, 57R, 58R)

✻ parchment or waxed paper

✻ scissors

✻ flower nail

✻ paper pastry bags (see page 25)

food colors of choice

edible ink pen (black)

PIPING SIMPLE 5-PETAL FLOWERS:

1 From a sheet of parchment paper, cut small squares slightly larger than the flower to be piped.

2 Make a paper pastry bag and snip the tip off the empty bag to produce an opening large enough to fit a metal piping tip. Drop a Wilton 104 or PME 58R piping tip inside the bag, narrow end first.

3 Fill the bag with appropriately colored stiff-peak icing.

4 Pipe a small dot of icing on top of the flower nail, stick one of the paper squares on top, and hold the nail in one hand.

5 Hold the pastry bag in the other hand at a 45-degree angle to the nail, with the wide end of the tip touching the middle of the flower nail and the narrow end pointing out and slightly raised.

6 Squeeze out the first petal and give the nail a one-quarter turn as you move the nozzle out toward the edge of the flower nail. Use less pressure as you are moving back toward the middle and curve the nozzle slightly to give the petal a natural shape. Stop squeezing as the wide end touches the middle of the nail and lift up the tip.

7 Repeat this 4 more times to make all the petals.

8 Remove the flower with its base paper from the nail and leave it to dry.

9 Pipe small yellow dots into the middle as stamens.

Note: for smaller flowers, simply use one of the smaller piping tips listed.

PIPING DAISIES:

1 Use a Wilton 104 piping tip and some stiff-peak white royal icing.

2 Prepare your pastry bag and paper squares for the flower nail as above.

3 Mark the middle of the paper-lined nail with a dot of icing.

4 Start at the outer edge of the nail, holding the wide end of the tip away from the middle and the narrow end towards the middle of the nail.

5 Slightly touch the paper with the wide end of the piping tip, squeeze out the icing and pull the tip toward the middle as you release the pressure. Stop and pull the tip away.

6 Repeat for 8 or more petals, while turning the nail appropriately (see below).

7 Remove the flower with the base paper from the nail and leave to dry.

8 Pipe small yellow dots into the middle as stamens.

Note: for smaller flowers, simply use one of the smaller piping tips.

PIPING PANSIES:

1 You will need 2 pastry bags with 2 piping tips of the same size, 1 filled with yellow and 1 filled with purple stiff-peak icing.

2 Start with the yellow icing. Pipe 2 petals next to each other following the same piping technique as for the simple 5-petal flower.

3 Repeat and pipe 2 shorter yellow petals on top of the larger ones.

4 For the large base petal, tuck the tip with the purple icing under the right side of the large yellow petal and start squeezing out a petal the same width as the 2 larger petals, using a back-and-forth hand motion for a ruffled effect.

5 Remove the flower with the paper from the nail and leave to dry.

6 Using a pen filled with edible black ink, draw fine lines into the middle of the pansy.

7 Pipe a fine yellow loop in the middle as a stamen.

PIPING DAFFODILS:

1 Using a PME 58R piping tip and egg-yellow stiff-peak icing, pipe a 6-petal flower on top of a paper-lined flower nail, using the same technique as for the daisy.

2 Remove the flower with the base paper from the nail and leave to dry.

3 Pipe 3 rings of pale orange icing on top of each other into the middle of the flower and let the icing dry.

4 Once dry, pipe a fine ruffled line over the edge of the circle.

marzipan roses ~~~~~~

I am a big fan of marzipan or sugar roses, but I do have to say it took me a while to master the perfect rose. You might also need a little practice until you are happy with your results.

FOR ABOUT 6 LARGE OR 12 SMALL ROSES OR 20 ROSEBUDS:

9 ounces neutral-colored marzipan or ready-to-use rolled fondant

pink food color

green food color

EQUIPMENT

* 2 sheets of cellophane
* small rolling pin
* rose calyx cutter
* rose leaf cutter
* leaf veiner

Color two-fifths of the marzipan pale pink, two-fifths dark pink and one-fifth green.

TO MAKE ROSEBUDS:

1 You will need 2 hazelnut-sized balls of dark pink marzipan and one twice as large.

2 Place these pieces of marzipan between 2 sheets of cellophane (see 1) and, starting with the larger one, push it down sideways to make it longer, and then flatten one long side with your thumb until very thin (see 2).

3 For the other petals, push a smaller ball down with your thumb, starting from the middle to one side, until it forms a round petal with one thick and one thin side. Repeat with the other.

4 Roll the large petal to a spiral shape, thin side up (see 3). This will form the middle of the rose.

5 Take one of the smaller petals, thin side up, and lay it around the middle over the seam (see 4).

6 Tuck the third petal slightly inside the second and squeeze it around the middle (see 5).

7 Slightly curve the petal edges out with your fingertips (see 6).

TO MAKE SMALL ROSES:

8 Continue by laying another 3 petals of the same size around the rosebud, each slightly overlapping.

9 Again, slightly curve the edge of the petals out with your fingertips.

TO MAKE LARGE ROSES:

10 Continue by laying another 5 petals of the same size around the rosebud, each slightly overlapping.

11 Slightly curve the edge of the petals out with your fingertips. To finish, pinch excess marzipan off the bottom.

TO MAKE CALYCES AND LEAVES:

12 Roll out some green marzipan between the 2 sheets of cellophane.

13 Cut a calyx out with the rose calyx cutter and stick it underneath the bottom of the rose. (Marzipan will stick to itself; for rolled fondant use a little bit of water.)

14 Pinch and shape the tips with your fingers as required.

15 Cut the leaves out with the rose leaf cutter.

16 Press in the rose leaf veiner (see 8) and shape slightly with your fingers for a natural look (see 9).

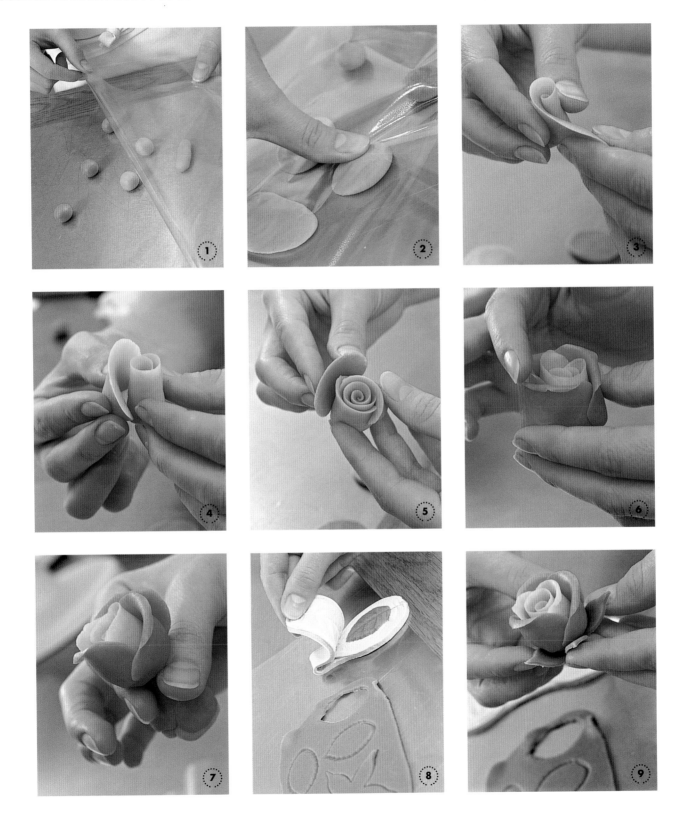

cookies

alphabet cookies

Alphabet cookies are very easy to make, even for beginners, as only the most basic of piping techniques are required. You can use the finished cookies to lay out names on your party table or arrange them into little messages, such as "HAPPY BIRTHDAY," "I LOVE YOU," "THANK YOU," "CONGRATULATIONS," and wrap them in beautiful gift boxes.

FOR ABOUT 10 TO 12 COOKIES

selection of food colors

about 1¼ cups royal icing (see page 24)

selection of 10 to 12 chocolate cookies
(see page 10), **made in letter shapes
of your choice**

EQUIPMENT

✻ **bowls**

✻ **small spatula for mixing**

✻ **paper pastry bags** (see page 25)

1 Choose your colors and prepare 1 pastry bag with soft-peak icing and another bag of runny icing in each color.

2 Using soft-peak icing, first pipe the outline of each cookie.

3 When you have finished, take the bag of runny icing in the same color and fill in the middles.

4 Leave the cookies to dry for about 1 hour before serving.

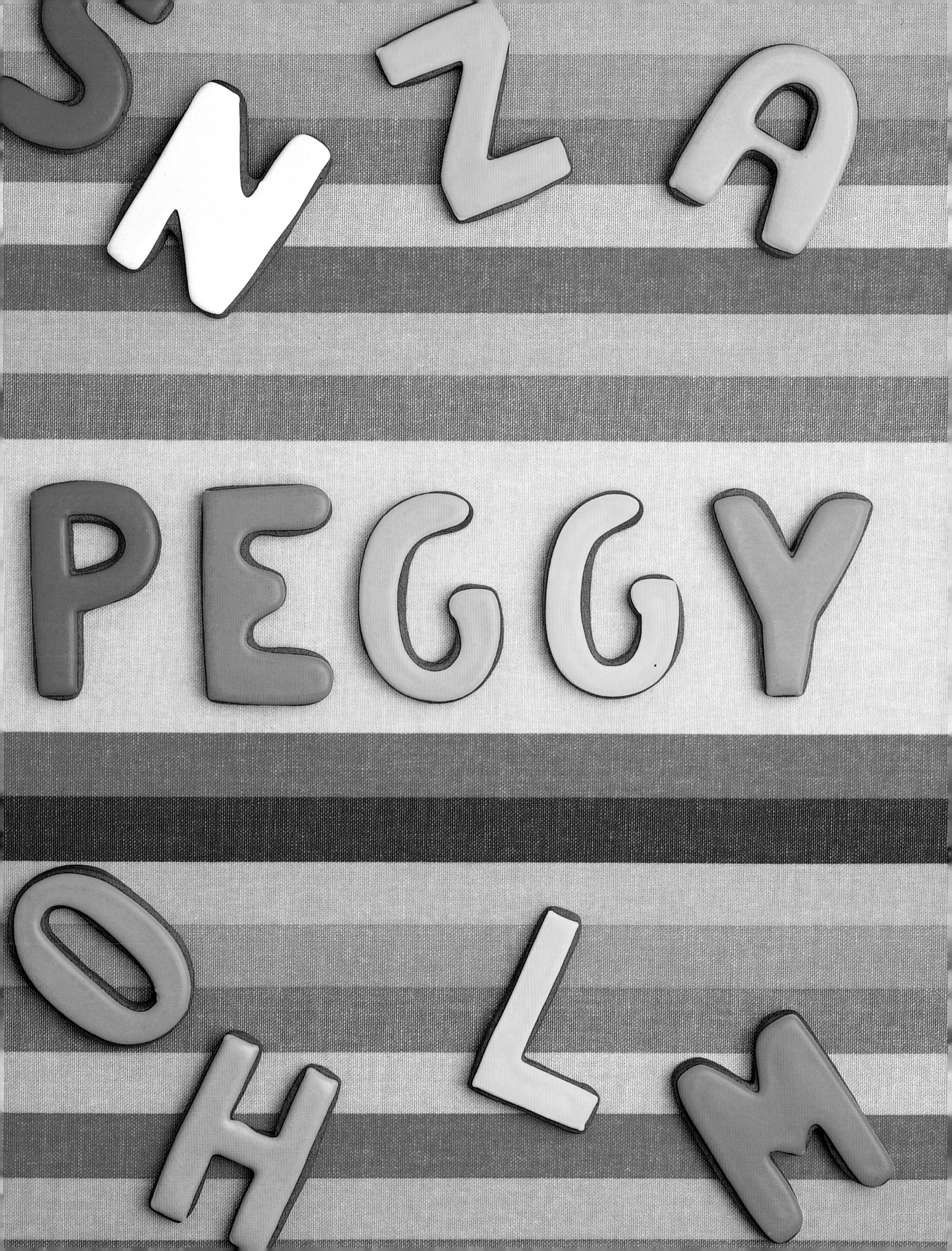
PEGGY

bollywood heart lollipops

It is simplicity itself to turn a simple shaped cookie into an attractive and fun lollipop by embedding a lollipop stick into the dough before baking. Decorated dramatically—here I've gone for Bollywood glamour, like the cupcakes on pages 66–7—they make the most charming gifts.

FOR 6 COOKIE LOLLIPOPS

food colors (yellow, orange, pink, blue, and purple)

1¼ cups royal icing (see page 24)

6 heart-shaped gingerbread cookies (see page 11) baked on a lollipop stick (see 1 and 2 above)

edible gold glitter

2 ounces pastel-pink rolled fondant

edible pink shimmer dust

EQUIPMENT

✳ bowls

✳ paper pastry bags (see page 25)

✳ small piece of parchment or waxed paper

✳ thin soft decorating brush

✳ push-in rose mold

✳ thick soft decorating brush

✳ 6 20-inch pieces organza ribbon in different colors

1 First mix your colors and prepare your pastry bags. You will need 1 bag of white soft-peak icing and 1 each of runny icing in bright yellow, orange, pink, blue, green (yellow + blue), and purple.

2 Using the white soft-peak icing, pipe the outline of the heart, then pipe dots evenly spaced around the outline (see 3).

3 Drizzle a layer of edible gold glitter on a piece of parchment or waxed paper and dip each cookie into the glitter while the outline icing is still wet. You want the outline and the dots completely covered with glitter; let dry.

4 Remove the excess glitter with a thin soft decorating brush (see 4).

5 Fill each heart with a different color of runny icing; let dry.

6 Shape a small piece of rolled fondant into a ball and push it into the rose mold (see 5). Remove it from the mold by bending the mold until the fondant comes out automatically. Repeat to make 5 more in the same way.

7 Using a thick soft decorating brush, dust the roses with the edible shimmer dust (see 6).

8 Stick 1 rose into the middle of each heart with a small dot of icing.

9 Fill a pastry bag with pastel-green soft-peak icing and snip off the tip in a "V" shape. Use to pipe small leaves around the roses; leave to dry.

10 Tie a piece of ribbon around the top of the lollipop stick.

flower basket cookies

A friend of mine once asked me for a gift idea for the flower girls at her wedding, so I came up with these flower basket cookies in the colors of the wedding flowers. Delicately wrapped in tissue paper and presented in a lovely gift box as shown on page 38, they also make a perfect little gift for Mother's Day or even just a little token to say "thank you" to someone.

FOR ABOUT 6 BASKET COOKIES AND 12 MINI FLOWER COOKIES

6 vanilla cookies (see page 10) **in the shape of a basket**

12 vanilla round cookies (see page 10), **about 1½ inches in diameter**

12 mini sugar flowers in each of three colors: pink, purple, and white (see pages 26–7)

2¼ cups royal icing (see page 24)

food colors (yellow, pink, purple)

EQUIPMENT

✳ **bowls**

✳ **small spatula**

✳ **paper pastry bags** (see page 25)

✳ **Wilton piping tip 103**

TO MAKE THE BASKETS:

1 First mix your colors and prepare your pastry bags. You will need 2 pastry bags filled with soft-peak icing, 1 in pastel pink, and the other in pastel purple, together with 2 pastry bags filled with runny icing in the same colors.

2 Using pink and purple soft-peak icing, pipe the outline of 3 baskets, including the handle, in each color.

3 Fill in the middle of each cookie with runny icing of the same color as the outline; let dry.

4 Stick 6 sugar flowers (2 of each color) into the middle of each basket and let them cascade down.

5 Finish the look by piping little green leaves next to the flowers as shown opposite.

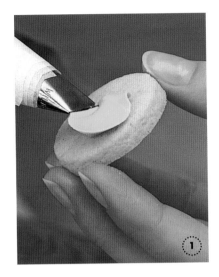

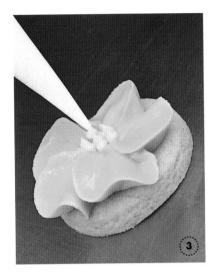

TO MAKE THE MINI FLOWER COOKIES:

To make a selection of pink, purple, and white flower cookies, follow the same technique as in Royal Iced Flowers on pages 26–7. Use the cookie as you would use the flower nail (without the paper, of course) and pipe the flower directly on it, using tip 103 (see 1–3). Once these are dry, snip a "V" shape from the tip of a paper pastry bag (see 4) and use it to pipe little green leaves around the flowers (see 5).

"a perfect little gift for Mother's Day"

underwater world

Loving everything about the ocean as I do, I was ecstatic when I came across this gorgeous set of waterworld cookie cutters. I couldn't wait to design bright multi-colored tropical fish, sea horses, and seashells. For this more grown-up version, I have kept the colors more subtle. The lobster, for example, can work well as a place card at a seafood-themed dinner party.

If you are making a selection of these cookies, first prepare all your colors and pastry bags. Then pipe all the cookie outlines first, so when you have finished with the last cookie, you can start filling in the middle of the first cookie. Continue in this way and you will save yourself a lot of time waiting for icing to dry.

FOR ABOUT 6 COOKIES

food colors (red, orange, brown, violet, dusky pink, blue, moss green, and yellow)

1¼ cups royal icing (see page 24)

6 gingerbread cookies (see page 11) in the shapes of a lobster, a tropical fish, a starfish, a sea horse, a seashell, and an octopus

EQUIPMENT

✳ bowl

✳ small spatula

✳ paper pastry bags (see page 25)

TO MAKE THE LOBSTER:

1 First prepare your colors and pastry bags. To make the red I used, mix your icing with red food color and a little bit of brown food color. You will need 1 bag of this in soft-peak icing. To make the orange, mix your icing with orange food color and a little bit of red food color. You will need 1 bag of this in soft-peak and another in runny icing.

2 Using the soft-peak orange icing, pipe the outline of the lobster.

3 Using the runny orange icing, fill in the middles; let dry.

4 Repeat the piping of the outlines, but this time using red icing. Also divide the body parts, give the lobster eyes, and add some detail to the tail; let dry.

TO MAKE THE TROPICAL FISH:

1 First prepare your colors and pastry bags. To make the green, mix your icing with moss-green food color and a little bit of yellow food color. You will need 1 bag of this in soft-peak icing and another in runny icing. You will also need 1 bag with yellow runny icing.

2 Using the green soft-peak icing, pipe the outlines, including the stripes of the fish.

3 Using green runny icing, fill in the face, the middle part of the fish and the tail; let dry.

4 Using the yellow runny icing, fill in the remaining parts; let dry.

5 Using the green soft-peak icing, repeat the piping of the outlines again, and add some detail to the fins.

6 Also pipe the eye using the yellow icing; let dry.

TO MAKE THE STARFISH:

1 First prepare your colors and pastry bags. To make the yellow, mix your icing with yellow food color and a little bit of brown food color. You will need 1 bag of this in soft-peak icing and another in runny icing. To make the orange, mix your icing with orange food color and a little bit of brown food color. You will need 1 bag of this in soft-peak icing.

2 Using the yellow soft-peak icing, pipe the outline of the starfish.

3 Using the yellow runny icing, fill in the middle; let dry.

4 Repeat the piping of the outline, but this time using the orange icing, and pipe some dots into the middle of the starfish; let dry.

TO MAKE THE SEA HORSE:

1 First prepare your colors and pastry bags. To make the blue, mix your icing with blue food color and a little bit of violet food color. You will need 1 bag of this in soft-peak icing and another in runny icing. To make the green, mix your icing with moss-green food color and yellow food color. You will need 1 bag of this in soft-peak icing.

2 Using the blue soft-peak icing, pipe the outline of the sea horse.

3 Using the runny blue icing, fill in the middle; let dry.

4 Using the green soft-peak icing, pipe the outline of the sea horse and give some detail to the body parts; let dry.

TO MAKE THE SEASHELL:

1 First prepare your colors and pastry bags. To make the pink, mix your icing with dusky-pink food color. You will need 1 bag of this in soft-peak icing and another in runny icing. To make the purple, mix your icing with violet food color and a little bit of dusky-pink food color. You will need 1 bag of this in runny icing.

2 Using the pink soft-peak icing, pipe the outline of the seashell. Also pipe a separation line for the purple front part of the shell.

3 Using the runny pink icing, fill in the main part of the shell; let dry.

4 Using the runny purple icing, fill in the small front part of the shell; let dry.

5 Using the soft-peak pink icing, pipe the outline and the individual sections again; let dry.

TO MAKE THE OCTOPUS:

1 First prepare your colors and pastry bags. To make the pink, mix your icing with dusky-pink food color and a bit of violet food color. You will need 1 bag of this in soft-peak icing. To make the purple, mix your icing with violet food color. You will need 1 bag of this in soft-peak and another in runny icing.

2 Using the purple soft-peak icing, pipe the outline of the octopus.

3 Using the purple runny icing, fill in the middle; let dry.

4 Using the pink soft-peak icing, pipe the outline again, and dots for the tentacles; let dry.

Easter egg cookies

When I was a child, I used to love painting Easter eggs with my mom each year. Making these cookies is also child's play, and a perfect thing to do if you are a beginner to decorating cookies. For an easy Easter gift you can even arrange a selection of eggs in various sizes with different designs in a suitably pretty basket and tie it with ribbon. See my Kaleidoscope Cakes on pages 64–5 for some more design ideas that also work well on egg-shaped cookies.

**FOR ABOUT 5 SMALL AND
5 LARGE COOKIES**

5 small and 5 large lemon cookies
(see page 10) **in egg shapes**
1¼ cups royal icing (see page 24)
selection of food colors

EQUIPMENT

✳ **bowls**
✳ **small spatula**
✳ **paper pastry bags** (see page 25)

1 Choose your background colors for your Easter egg cookies and prepare 1 bag of soft-peak and 1 bag of runny icing in each color.

2 First pipe all the outlines, using the soft-peak icing.

3 Fill the middles with the runny icing, using the same color as for the outlines; let set for about 1 hour.

4 Choose your colors for the decoration and start decorating the eggs with stripes and wavy lines using soft-peak icing; for dots, use thinned-down soft-peak icing.

birthday razzle dazzle

Decorating cookies is one of my favorite things to do as it is actually a lot easier than it looks. Create your own style, but keep your cookies smart and simple. Colorful patterns of dots and stripes piped on a plain background make very effective designs. You can either use these as a treat for guests at your own party—for instance, they make excellent place cards with guests' names written on them—or take them as gifts to a birthday party, presented stylishly gift-wrapped.

FOR ABOUT 10 TO 12 COOKIES

selection of 10 to 12 cookies (see page 10) shaped like gift boxes and birthday cakes

about 1¾ cups royal icing (see page 24)

selection of food colors

EQUIPMENT

* small spatula

* paper pastry bags (see page 25)

FOR THE GIFT BOXES

1 First spread on the background color: fill 1 pastry bag with soft-peak royal icing and 1 with runny.

2 Using soft-peak icing, pipe the outline of the box and let set briefly. With a bag of runny icing, fill in middle; let dry at least half an hour. Repeat with the remaining cookies.

3 Pick a color for the bow and fill 1 piping bag with soft-peak and 1 with runny icing in that color. Pipe the outline with soft-peak icing and, once that sets, fill in the middle with runny icing; let dry.

4 Once the icing is completely dry, pipe the outline and the lines marking the individual sections once more to create a 3-D look.

FOR THE BIRTHDAY CAKES

5 Again, start with a background color (white this time). Pipe the outline using soft-peak icing. Once set, fill in the middle with runny icing and let dry. Pipe the outline and the lines marking "tiers" again.

6 Choose colors and decoration and prepare pastry bags. For stripes, use soft-peak icing; for dots, thin down soft-peak icing with a little water to make it slightly runny.

7 Decorate the "sides" with stripes or dots. Pipe a few candles on the "top" with yellow icing for flames.

baby shower

What a perfect—and very personal gift—these will make for your best friend's baby shower. Wrap your selection of cute baby-themed cookies in an attractive presentation tin or box lined with tissue paper and tie it with a beautiful matching satin ribbon. If you already know the baby's name, why not pipe it on top of one of the cookies? If you don't know whether the baby is a girl or a boy, just make a mix of pink, blue, and yellow iced cookies.

FOR ABOUT 8 COOKIES

8 vanilla cookies (see page 10) in the shapes of a building block, a baby's bib, a stroller, a baby's bottle, a baby sleep suit, 2 booties, and a rattle

1¼ cups royal icing (see page 24)

food colors (pink, baby blue, yellow)

EQUIPMENT

* bowls
* small spatula
* paper pastry bags (see page 25)

First prepare your colors and pastry bags. You will need 1 bag of soft-peak icing in each color, 2 pastry bags of runny white, 1 of runny blue icing, and 1 small bag of runny yellow icing.

TO MAKE THE BUILDING BLOCK:

1 Using white soft-peak icing, pipe a white outline.

2 Using runny white icing, fill in the middle and let dry.

3 Using the blue soft-peak icing, pipe the outline again and the sides of the block, as well as the outlines for the alphabet letters.

4 Using runny blue icing, fill in the middles of the alphabet letters and let dry.

TO MAKE THE BABY'S BIB:

1 Using blue soft-peak icing, pipe the outline for the bow.

2 Using white soft-peak icing, pipe the outline for the bib.

3 Using blue runny icing, fill in the middle of the bow; let dry.

4 Using white runny icing, fill in the middle of the bib; let dry.

5 Using blue soft-peak icing, pipe the lines of the bow again.

6 Using white soft-peak icing, pipe the outline of the bib again; let dry.

"pink, blue, and yellow suits girls and boys"

TO MAKE THE STROLLER:

1 Using white soft-peak icing, pipe the outline of the hood.

2 Using blue soft-peak icing, pipe the outline of the rest of the stroller.

3 Using white runny icing, fill in the middle of the hood.

4 Using blue runny icing, fill in the rest of the stroller; let dry.

5 Using white soft-peak icing, pipe all the outlines again, and the wheels, as well as adding some detail to the stroller hood; let dry.

TO MAKE THE BABY'S BOTTLE:

1 Using white soft-peak icing, pipe the outline for the bottle.

2 Using blue soft-peak icing, pipe the outline for the top in blue.

3 Using yellow soft-peak icing, pipe the outline for the nipple; let dry.

4 Fill in the middles with runny icing using the same colors; let dry.

5 Pipe the outlines of the individual parts again using the same soft-peak icing as before.

6 Using white soft-peak icing, pipe an ounce scale on the front of the bottle; let dry.

TO MAKE THE BABY SLEEP SUIT:
Follow the same procedure as for the booties (above right), piping the outline first, then fill in the middle and pipe the dots. Finish by repeating the outline and piping some details of the suit.

TO MAKE THE BOOTIES:

1 Using white soft-peak icing, pipe the outlines for the booties.

2 Using white runny icing, fill in the middles.

3 While that is still wet, use blue runny icing to pipe small dots all over the booties, so they level out with the white icing. Leave everything to dry.

4 Using blue soft-peak icing, pipe the blue ribbon bow.

6 Using white soft-peak icing, pipe the outline of the booties again; let dry.

TO MAKE THE RATTLE:
Follow the same procedure as for the booties, piping the outline first, then fill in the middle and pipe the dots for the bow. Finish by repeating the outlines and details of the bow.

butterfly cookies

The challenge is to find the butterflies... this is just one of many examples of how an attractive piece of printed fabric can instantly inspire you into creating something simply gorgeous, like these brilliant little butterflies. Use these for a summer tea party or picnic lunch.

FOR ABOUT 10 COOKIES

choice of food color (here pastel pink)

1¼ cups royal icing (see page 24)

10 vanilla cookies in butterfly shape
  (see page 10)

EQUIPMENT

* bowls

* small spatula

* paper pastry bags (see page 25)

1 Prepare 1 pastry bag of white soft-peak icing for the outline and the body, and 1 pastry bag of runny pastel-pink icing for filling in the middle. For piping the little dots, thin down bright pink soft-peak icing with a little bit of water to make it slightly runny, and put in a third bag.

2 Start by piping the white outline of the wings.

3 Once the outlines are set, fill in the wing middles with the pastel-pink icing. Leave these to dry for about half an hour.

4 Once the wings have dried, snip the tip of the pastry bag containing the white icing to make it slightly larger and pipe the body between the wings, starting from the top and pulling it down toward you.

5 Finally, pipe little dots all over the wings, using your bright pink runny icing.

cookie catwalk

As if they have just come from the latest fashion shows in Paris or New York, you can create your own cookie catwalk to reflect the season's latest trends and colors, using nothing more than the tip of a pastry bag and some appropriately colored icing.

FOR ABOUT 12 COOKIES

12 chocolate cookies (see page 10) in the shape of handbags, dresses, and shoes

2¼ cups royal icing (see page 24)

food colors (chocolate brown, pink)

EQUIPMENT

＊ bowl

＊ small spatula

＊ paper pastry bags (see page 25)

First prepare your colors and pastry bags. You will need 1 bag of soft-peak icing in each color and 3 or 4 pastry bags of runny icing in each color.

TO MAKE THE HANDBAGS:

1 Using soft-peak icing in your color of choice, pipe the outline of the body of the handbag.

2 Fill in the middle with runny icing of the same color as the outline; let dry.

3 Using soft-peak icing of a different color, repeat the piping of the outline and add details like a bow and the handbag handle; let dry.

TO MAKE THE SHOES:

1 Using soft-peak icing in your color of choice, pipe the outline of the shoe.

2 Fill in the middle with runny icing of the same color as the outline; let dry.

3 Using soft-peak icing of the same color, repeat the outline and add details like a bow or a dot

design in a different color. For dot designs, pipe dots into the still-soft icing (see Baby Booties, page 50); for bows, wait until the basic color underneath has set.

TO MAKE THE DRESSES:

1 For full dresses outline, fill in, and decorate the cookies using the same techniques as above.

2 For 2-piece outfits, outline the top and the skirt separately using soft-peak icing in 2 different colors.

3 Fill in the top first and let dry. Then fill in the skirt and let that dry.

4 Repeat the outlining of the cookies using the same icing, and add small details like collars, belts or bows; let dry.

5 For dot designs, pipe dots into the still-soft icing (see Baby Booties, page 50); for collars, belts, or bows, wait until the basic color underneath has set.

snowflake cookies

These sparkly little jewels are easy to make and will add a magical touch to any Christmas party. To turn them into strikingly original tree ornaments, simply poke a hole into the cookies before you bake them, then hang them up using pieces of satin ribbon.

FOR ABOUT 6 COOKIES

2¼ cups royal icing (see page 24)

6 gingerbread cookies (see page 11) in the shape of snowflakes

white edible glitter

EQUIPMENT

✳ bowls

✳ small spatula

✳ paper pastry bags (see page 25)

1 First prepare your icing bags. Fill 1 with white soft-peak icing and 2 with white runny icing.

2 Pipe the outline of the cookie, including the design in the middle.

3 Using white runny icing, fill in the middle.

4 While still wet, drizzle white glitter generously over the icing until completely covered; let dry.

5 Before use, shake off any excess glitter.

cupcakes

cupcake garden

As the name might suggest, these cupcakes can be decorated with any kind of flower you choose. Make a variety of the sugar flowers as shown on pages 26–7 and place one on each cake. (Here we've used the simple 5-petal flowers only.) For an attractive and original table centerpiece, you can easily arrange some of these cakes on a pretty cake stand and then adorn them with some fresh flowers from your garden—or the florist.

FOR ABOUT 25 CUPCAKES

25 pink 5-petal sugar flowers
(see page 26)

25 chocolate cupcakes (made using ½ recipe quantity basic sheet cake batter, see page 12, baked in silver paper cases)

¾ cup plain sugar syrup (see page 15)

generous 1 cup chocolate ganache
(see page 15)

½ cup royal icing (see page 24)

green food color

EQUIPMENT

✳ pastry brush

✳ small spatula

✳ paper pastry bag (see page 25)

✳ scissors

1 Make the sugar flowers a day in advance, as described on page 26.

2 Using a pastry brush, soak the tops of the cupcakes with the sugar syrup.

3 Using a small spatula, ice the cupcakes with chocolate ganache; let set.

4 Place 1 sugar blossom on top of each cupcake, fixing in place with a little drop of ganache.

5 Mix the royal icing with some green food color and put it in the pastry bag. Cut a "V" shape in the tip of the bag and pipe some leaves around the flower. (See Flower Basket Cookies, page 36.)

daisy dot cupcakes

The decoration of sweet daisies, looking so pure and innocent, makes these pretty cupcakes ideal for engagement parties, a little girl's birthday party, or other celebration, but they can also serve as adorable treats for people of all types and ages—especially keen gardeners.

FOR ABOUT 12 CUPCAKES

7 ounces white gum paste

a little vegetable shortening

confectioners' sugar for dusting

yellow food color

superfine sugar for dipping

a little royal icing (see page 24)

12 vanilla cupcakes, iced with
fondant icing (see pages 20–23)
in pastel colors (made using ¼
recipe quantity sheet cake batter,
see page 12)

EQUIPMENT

* small plastic board
* daisy cutter
* small spatula
* foam pad
* Cel Stick or toothpick
* painter's palette
* small rolling pin
* decorating brush
* paper pastry bag (see page 25)

1 Make the sugar daisies at least 1 day ahead. Knead the gum paste with a little shortening until smooth and pliable.

2 Roll out a walnut-size piece of paste on a plastic board until very thin. If it sticks to the board, grease the board lightly with the shortening.

3 Press the daisy cutter firmly on the paste and cut out the shape (see 1). Carefully lift with a spatula and lay on the foam pad.

4 Roll the Cel Stick or toothpick gently back and forth over each petal as shown to shape it (see 2).

5 Dust a painter's palette with confectioners' sugar and place the

flower over one of the wells. Push the middle down gently with the end of the rolling pin (see 3).

6 Mix a small bead of flower gum paste with a drop of yellow food color and shape to a ball. Brush lightly with water and dip in sugar. Stick in the middle of the daisy with a little water. Repeat to make 12 daisies; let dry overnight.

DECORATE THE CUPCAKES:

7 Pipe a dot of royal icing on top of each cupcake and stick a daisy on it.

8 Finish by piping little dots of white icing all over the tops.

bollywood kitsch cakes

As the name suggests, the idea for these cakes came to me when Bollywood turned into high fashion and Andrew Lloyd Webber's glittering musical *Bombay Dreams* premiered, inspiring me to make these sparkling edible jewels.

FOR ABOUT 30 FONDANT FANCIES

30 fondant fancies (made as described on pages 22–3, using 1 recipe quantity basic sheet cake batter and bright pink, yellow, orange, turquoise, and purple fondant icing)

15 small pink marzipan roses (see page 28)

45 small pink marzipan rosebuds (see page 28)

90 small green marzipan rose leaves (see page 28)

pink and green edible glitter

½ cup soft-peak royal icing (see page 24)

edible gold shimmer dust

1 tablespoon clear alcohol, such as vodka

EQUIPMENT

✳ about 30 golden paper cases

✳ small spatula

✳ paper pastry bags (see page 25)

✳ scissors

✳ fine decorating brush

1 Put the fondant fancies in golden paper cases.

2 Make the roses, rosebuds, and leaves as described on page 28. While the marzipan is still wet, dip the flowers in the pink glitter and the leaves in the green glitter.

3 Put the soft-peak royal icing into a paper pastry bag and pipe fine swirls or dots on top of the fondant fancies as shown (see 1); let dry.

4 Mix some gold shimmer dust to a paste with a drop of clear alcohol and use the decorating brush to color the swirls and dots with it (see 2).

5 Stick the roses and leaves into the middle of each cake using a dab of royal icing (see 3).

hot hearts

These sparkling little heart cakes, which are very simple and easy to make, are completely adorable. Surprise the love of your life with this edible token of your devotion at a Valentine's Day dinner, or use them as treats at a wedding or engagement party.

FOR ABOUT 30

30 heart-shaped fondant fancies
   (made as described on pages 22–3,
   using red and pink fondant icing
   and 1 recipe quantity sheet cake
   batter, see page 12)
red and pink edible glitter
1 tablespoon clear alcohol, such as
   vodka

EQUIPMENT

✳ about 30 silver paper cases
✳ parchment or waxed paper
✳ decorating brush

1 While the fondant icing on the fancies is still slightly wet, place each heart fancy in a silver paper case, hold between both hands as shown, and push the paper case against the sides until it sticks to the cake (see 1).

2 Sprinkle a thick layer of each type of glitter on a small piece of parchment or waxed paper.

3 Brush each red heart thinly with the clear alcohol and dip into the red glitter (see 2). Do the same with the pink hearts and the pink glitter.

christmas trees

These little dazzlers provide a modern and elegant approach to traditional festive celebrations. The soft contrast of sparkling snow-white trees on an icy pine-green background make these cakes look effortlessly stylish. You can, of course, do the reverse to great effect.

FOR ABOUT 30

1¼ cups royal icing (see page 24)

edible white glitter

30 fondant fancies, cut in 1- x 2-inch rectangles (as described on pages 22–3, using pastel-green fondant and 1 recipe quantity sheet cake batter, see page 12)

EQUIPMENT

* small amount of vegetable shortening
* sheet of cellophane
* template with small tree shapes (see page 140)
* paper pastry bags (see page 25)
* small spatula

1 Make the royal icing trees at least 2 days in advance. Place the cellophane on top of the tree template and rub a very thin layer of shortening over it with your hand so the icing doesn't stick.

2 Fill 1 piping bag with soft-peak white royal icing and 1 bag with runny white royal icing.

3 Using the soft-peak icing, first pipe the outlines of the trees on the cellophane (see 1).

4 Fill the middles of the trees with the runny icing (see 2) and, while still wet, sprinkle white glitter over the trees (see 3).

5 Let dry in a warm place for 2 days.

6 Once they are dry, lift them from the cellophane with a spatula and stick them on top of the fondant fancies using a dot of royal icing.

ruffle rose cupcakes

I saw this gorgeously girly cakestand in a department store while I was on a trip to New York, and I just had to have it. Here its romantic ruffle design provides the perfect setting for my wild rose cupcakes, which were inspired by it.

FOR ABOUT 25 CUPCAKES

25 vanilla cupcakes (made using
½ recipe quantity sheet cake batter,
see page 12, baked in white paper
cases)

¾ cup vanilla sugar syrup (see page 15)

2¼ cups vanilla buttercream
(see page 14)

75 small dusky pink marzipan roses
(3 per cupcake, see page 28)

150 small moss-green marzipan
leaves (6 per cupcake, see page 28)

EQUIPMENT

* pastry brush
* small spatula

1 Using the pastry brush, soak the tops of the cupcakes with the sugar syrup.

2 Using the spatula, cover the tops with the buttercream.

3 Place the roses and the leaves on top of the cakes, pressing them slightly into the buttercream to fix them in place.

4 Ideally, arrange them on a beautiful old-fashioned cakestand.

butterfly fancies

If you want to add a real touch of magic to your party, you can't go wrong with these delicate butterfly fancies. Don't they just look as if they want to fly away? Be careful, though, you'd better keep an eye on them...Perhaps it would be better to eat them first.

FOR ABOUT 25 FANCIES

small amount of vegetable shortening

food colors (pink, orange, yellow, and blue)

1½ cups royal icing (see page 24)

25 small fondant fancies, 1½ inches square (made as described on pages 22–3, using about ½ recipe quantity basic sheet cake batter and using fondant icing in several different candy colors)

EQUIPMENT

∗ sheet of cellophane

∗ butterfly templates (see page 140–1)

∗ paper pastry bags (see page 25)

∗ thin cardboard

∗ parchment or waxed paper

∗ scissors

∗ small spatula

∗ 25 silver cupcake cases

Prepare the butterflies at least 2 days in advance. Place the cellophane on top of the butterfly templates and rub a thin layer of shortening on top with your hands to prevent the icing from sticking.

TO MAKE THE YELLOW BUTTERFLY:

1 Mix your colors and prepare your pastry bags. You will need 1 pastry bag filled with soft-peak yellow icing, another with soft-peak pale-blue icing, and a third with runny yellow icing.

2 Using the soft-peak yellow icing, pipe the outline of the butterfly.

3 Using the runny yellow icing, fill the top wings, and let them dry.

4 Using the same icing, fill the bottom wings and let dry.

5 Using soft-peak pale-blue icing, pipe the little blue dots on top as shown.

TO MAKE THE BLUE BUTTERFLY:

1 Mix your colors and prepare your pastry bags. You will need 1 bag filled with soft-peak blue icing, another with soft-peak green (yellow plus blue) icing, and a third with runny blue icing.

2 Using the soft-peak blue icing, pipe the outline of the butterfly.

3 Using the runny blue icing, fill the top wings and let them dry.

4 Using the same icing, fill the bottom wings and let dry.

5 Using soft-peak green icing, pipe the little green dots on top as shown.

TO MAKE THE GREEN BUTTERFLY:

1 Mix your colors and prepare your pastry bags. You will need 1 bag filled with soft-peak bright-green icing, another with runny bright-green icing, and a third with runny light-green icing.

2 Using the soft-peak bright-green icing, pipe the outline of the butterfly.

3 Using the runny bright-green icing, fill the top wings, and let them dry.

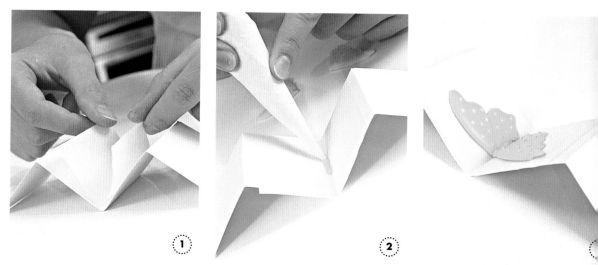

4 Using the runny light-green icing, fill the bottom wings and let dry.

TO MAKE THE PINK BUTTERFLY:

1 Mix your colors and prepare your pastry bags. You will need 1 bag filled with soft-peak pale-pink icing, another with runny pale-pink icing, and a third with runny bright-pink icing.

2 Using the pale-pink soft-peak icing, pipe the outline of the butterfly.

3 Using the same icing, pipe a parallel line just inside the wing outline, leaving a small border.

4 Using the runny pale-pink icing, fill the gap between these outlines.

5 Using the runny bright-pink icing, fill the middles; let dry.

TO MAKE THE ORANGE BUTTERFLY:

1 Mix your colors and prepare your pastry bags. You will need 1 bag filled with soft-peak yellow icing, another with runny yellow icing, and a third with runny orange icing.

2 Using the yellow soft-peak icing, pipe the outline of the butterfly.

3 Using the same icing, pipe an inner line outline and dots, leaving a border.

4 Using the runny orange icing, fill the main middles of the wings; let dry.

5 Using the runny yellow icing, fill the outside border and the dots; let dry.

TO FINISH ALL THE BUTTERFLIES:

1 Pipe a couple of feelers for each butterfly in a matching color on a piece of parchment or waxed paper.

2 Let everything dry and set for at least 2 days in a warm dry place.

3 Fold some pieces of thin cardboard to a "V" shape to support the wings and line with a piece of folded parchment or waxed paper (see 1).

4 Pipe a small line of royal icing in a color matching the butterfly into the fold of the paper (see 2). Lift the wings with the small spatula and place them in position on either side of the "V" shape (see 3). Let the butterflies dry in position for at least 3 hours.

5 Put the fondant fancies in silver cupcake cases and stick a butterfly on top of each with a dot of stiff-peak royal icing (see 4 and 5).

6 Using soft-peak icing in appropriate colors, pipe a head and a body in the middle between the wings (see 6) and stick 2 feelers carefully into the head (see 7).

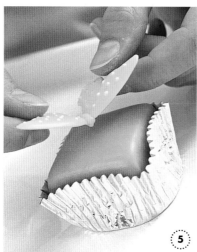

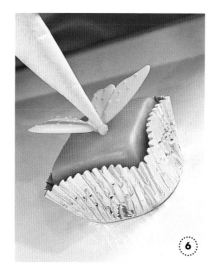

pansy pots

My parents, both dedicated hobby gardeners, were undoubtedly the inspiration for these adorable little cakes, as pansies are high on their list of favorite flowers. Whenever I go back home in spring, our garden is just full of their brilliant colors. It's no surprise, then, that I felt compelled to turn their passion into sweet treats as gifts for them. Make these cakes at least a day before you need them. The pansy flowers can be made well in advance, as they last for weeks.

FOR 12 CAKES

butter and flour for lining the molds

¼ recipe quantity chocolate cake batter (see page 12)

1¼ cups plain sugar syrup (see page 15)

18 ounces white ready-to-use rolled fondant

food colors (brown, orange, pink, yellow, violet, moss green)

1 teaspoon Tylose powder (see step 6)

10 ounces white gum paste

small amount of vegetable shortening

2½ tablespoons apricot jam, strained

9 ounces chocolate-flavored ready-to-use rolled fondant

½ cup royal icing (see page 24)

EQUIPMENT

* 12 timbale molds
* wire cooling rack
* pastry brush
* plastic wrap
* small plastic board
* pansy petal and leaf cutters
* foam pad
* bone tool
* fine decorating brush
* small painter's palette
* black edible ink pen
* small rolling pin
* small kitchen knife
* leaf veining mat
* paper pastry bag (see page 25)

1 To bake the cakes, preheat the oven to 350°F. Grease 12 timbale molds with butter and dust them with flour, shaking out excess.

2 Make the cake batter as described on page 12 and then spoon it into the prepared timbale molds just enough to half fill them only.

3 Bake for about 15 minutes. Leave the cakes to cool a little on a wire rack and then turn them out of their molds (see page 85).

4 To make the flowerpots, once the cakes are cool, soak their tops with the sugar syrup using a pastry brush, wrap them in plastic wrap, and chill for at least 2 hours to firm them up.

5 Mix the white rolled fondant with some brown and orange food color until you achieve a nice terracotta color.

6 Mix in the Tylose powder. (This is a hardening agent that will also help to make the paste more flexible and stable.) Wrap the fondant in plastic wrap and leave to rest for at least half an hour.

7 While the fondant is resting, make the pansy flowers. Divide the white gum paste into 7 pieces. Keep 1 piece white and color the remaining pieces with yellow, moss green, 2 different shades of pink, and violet. Wrap the ones you aren't going to use immediately in plastic wrap to prevent them from drying out.

8 Rub a thin layer of vegetable shortening over a plastic board to prevent the gum paste from sticking to it.

9 Roll out 1 color of paste very thinly and, using a pansy petal cutter, cut out the petals. For 1 blossom you will need 2 large and 2 small teardrop-shape petals and 1 large base petal as shown.

10 Place the petals on the foam pad and smooth the edges by using the bone tool (see 4).

11 Arrange the petals into a flower by placing the 2 small petals next to each other, slightly overlapping, and stick them together by brushing the sides where they touch with a little bit of water. Place the 2 large petals to the left and to the right below the small petals, also overlapping and touching the sides. Use a little water to stick them to the small petals. Finally stick on the large base petal with a little bit of water (see 5) and push a little well into the middle, using the end of a brush or a pointed flower tool (see 6).

12 Place the flower into the well of a small painter's palette to let it dry (see 7). Repeat the procedure for all the flowers; you will need 6 flowers per pot.

13 Depending on the thickness of your paste, let the flowers dry for at least 2 to 4 hours.

14 Once they are dry, paint some fine black lines into the middle using a black edible ink pen.

15 When the cakes are chilled, bring the jam to a boil in a small pan, turn the cakes upside-down, and brush the sides and tops with jam.

16 Roll out the terracotta fondant to about ⅛ inch thick and lay it over the upside-down cakes. Using a kitchen knife, trim off the excess fondant and let the iced cakes set for at least 4 hours, until the fondant feels firm to the touch (see 1).

17 Turn the cakes back over. Roll out some more of the terracotta fondant to the same thickness as before and cut out 12 strips each ⅜ inch wide and about 6 inches long. (They dry out very quickly, so it is best to work on 3 or 4 at a time.)

18 Brush the top edge of each pot with a little bit of water and stick the terracotta strip around it (see 2). If the strip is too long, trim off the excess with a small knife.

19 Roll a piece of chocolate-flavored rolled fondant into a ball

and flatten it to a slight dome shape large enough to cover the cake still showing inside the pot.

20 Brush the cake with hot jam and stick the rolled fondant on top (see 3).

21 Before sticking the flowers on top of the pot, make the pansy leaves. Mix some of the gum paste with moss-green food color and roll it out very thinly.

22 Cut out the leaves using a metal leaf cutter and place them on the foam pad.

23 Use the bone tool to smooth the edges and the veining mat to give them veins (see 8).

24 Stick the flowers and leaves on top of the flowerpots with little dabs of royal icing. While they are still soft, shape the leaves and make sure you have hardly any gaps between the flowers and the leaves (see 9).

MAKING THE PANSY POTS

"our garden is just full of their brilliant colors"

mini tea rose wedding cakes

Miniature wedding cakes provide a modern twist to the traditional large cake and are ideal for smaller wedding receptions. Instead of having one large cake to cut, the bride and groom can serve individual cakes to each of their guests. This particular cake is inspired by the lovely ceramic artistry of the tea set on which it is served. Begin the cakes at least a day in advance. The flowers can be made well before you need them, as they will last for weeks.

FOR ABOUT 6 CAKES

1 sheet of layer cake, 12 x 16 inches, using 1 recipe quantity basic sheet cake batter, flavored and soaked to your choice (see page 12–13)

⅓ cup apricot jam, strained

confectioners' sugar for dusting

18 ounces white ready-to-use rolled fondant

2 ounces ready-to-use rolled fondant

violet food color

¼ cup royal icing (see page 24)

edible gold shimmer dust

1 teaspoon clear alcohol, such as vodka

30 mini roses made from rolled fondant colored dusky pink (see pages 26–9)

36 rose leaves made from moss-green rolled fondant (see pages 26–9)

EQUIPMENT

* plastic wrap
* round cookie cutters, 3 inches and 1½ inches in diameter
* small saucepan
* pastry brush
* small rolling pin
* ¼-inch guide sticks
* 2 fondant smoothers
* small kitchen knife
* parchment or waxed paper
* small plastic board
* miniature blossom cutter
* bone tool
* paper pastry bags (see page 25)
* fine decorating brush

1 Wrap the soaked sheet of cake in plastic wrap and chill for about 2 hours until firm.

2 Using 3-inch and 1½-inch round cookie cutters, cut out 6 circles in each size from the firmed-up cake.

3 Bring the jam to a boil in a small pan and, using a pastry brush, brush each circle all over with the hot jam.

4 On a counter top dusted with confectioners' sugar, roll out the white fondant paste to ¼ inch thick using guide sticks and cover each of the circles with the fondant, as described on page 17.

5 Use the fondant smoothers to straighten the sides and tops of each of the cakes.

6 Trim off excess fondant using a small kitchen knife, place the cakes on a sheet of parchment or waxed paper, and let set for a day.

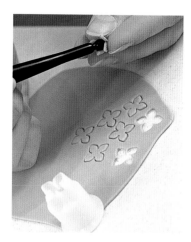

7 Make the lilac blossoms by mixing the 2 ounces of rolled fondant with a little violet food color. Roll out thinly on a plastic board dusted with confectioners' sugar. Cut out the blossoms using a mini blossom cutter and shape with a bone tool as shown; let dry overnight.

8 Pipe a small dot of royal icing in the middle of each of the large cakes and then place a small cake on top.

9 Pipe a border (see page 25) around the bottom of each tier and let it dry.

10 Mix some gold shimmer dust to a paste with a little bit of clear alcohol and paint the piped border using a fine decorating brush.

11 Stick the lilac blossoms, mini roses, and leaves on top of the cake with little dabs of royal icing.

treasure boxes

These little sugar boxes make exclusive keepsakes for special occasions. The design is inspired by my favorite tableware, Follement by Christian Lacroix. Finished with lavishly formed golden handles, they look more like treasure boxes. You need good piping skills and some patience to make these. If you're worried that these designs are a bit too difficult for you, keep the look simple. Dust the entire box with one color and use a marzipan rose (see page 28–9) for the handle.

FOR ABOUT 6 BOXES

10 ounces white ready-to-use rolled fondant

1 teaspoon Tylose Powder (see page 83)

1 egg white

confectioners' sugar for dusting

a little vegetable shortening

edible shimmer dust (gold, pink blue, green, and yellow)

a little clear alcohol, such as vodka

a little royal icing (see page 24)

EQUIPMENT

* plastic wrap
* round bottle or can
* piece of cardboard
* small rolling pin
* ¼-inch guide sticks
* small kitchen knife
* several fine decorating brushes
* tray
* round cookie cutters
* paper pastry bags (see page 25)

1 Begin the boxes at least 3 days before you need them. Mix the rolled fondant with the Tylose Powder to make a modeling paste. Wrap in plastic wrap and allow to rest for 15 minutes.

2 Choose a bottle that will make a good template. Cut a rectangular piece of cardboard about 2½ inches wide and long enough to wrap around the bottle. Using guide sticks, roll a piece of paste out to a thickness of ⅛ inch and, using the template, cut out a strip that size (see 1 on following page). Brush the end of the strip lightly with egg white. Dust the paste with confectioners' sugar and wrap around the bottle (see 2 on following page). Carefully squeeze the ends together to stick. Move to a tray dusted with confectioners' sugar. Carefully remove the bottle and leave the cylinder to dry overnight.

3 To make the lid, roll another piece of modeling paste out to the same thickness and use a suitably sized cutter to stamp out a lid. Leave to dry on the tray overnight.

4 To make the handles, roll a piece of paste into a thin log and shape it into swirls and curls; let dry overnight.

5 Next day, roll out a small piece of paste as before. Brush the edge of one end of the paste cylinder

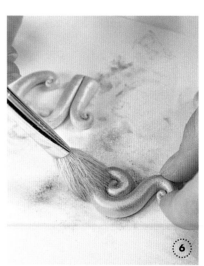

with a little egg white and place firmly on the paste so it sticks. With a sharp knife, cut around the edge to leave the new base in place (see 3). Place the box, bottom side down, on a tray that has been dusted with confectioners' sugar and leave to dry overnight.

6 Next day, fill a pastry bag with soft-peak royal icing and pipe swirls and waves on the box and the lid (see 4); let dry for an hour.

7 Once dry, using a fine brush, apply a thin layer of shortening to parts you want to color. Using another clean dry brush, dust these with the edible shimmer dust (see 5).

8 Mix a small amount of gold shimmer dust to a paste with a drop of alcohol. Use to paint the piped lines and the handle (see 6).

9 Brush the handles with a little shortening and dust with shimmer dust using a brush (see 6).

10 Pipe a dot of royal icing in the middle of the lid and stick the handle on top; let dry for 2 hours.

swirly whirly cakes

These crazy little swirly party cakes were inspired by an ultra-cool piece of fabric that grabbed my eye in the window of a store near my house. I often find fabrics, wallpapers, and china services provide fabulous sources of inspiration. I just love to wander through interior and ceramic stores in hope of finding something special that will spark off a new idea. These are nice and easy for beginners to make—or even for getting the children to help.

FOR ABOUT 12 TO 15 CAKES

1 sheet of chocolate cake 12 x16 inches, using 1 recipe quantity basic sheet cake batter (see page 12)

1¼ cups sugar syrup, flavored to your choice (see page 15)

1 generous cup chocolate ganache (see page 15)

confectioners' sugar for dusting

1¼ pounds chocolate-flavored ready-to-use rolled fondant

10 ounces white ready-to-use rolled fondant

selection of food colors

½ cup soft-peak royal icing (see page 24)

EQUIPMENT

* bread knife and small kitchen knife
* pastry brush
* plastic wrap
* selection of round biscuit cutters
* small spatula
* rolling pin
* ¼-inch guide sticks
* 2 fondant smoothers
* selection of different-colored satin ribbon, ½ inch wide
* scissors

1 Trim the cake and soak it with the syrup using a pastry brush. Wrap in plastic wrap and chill for about 2 hours until firm.

2 Once the cake is firm, use the biscuit cutters to cut out a variety of round miniature cakes in different sizes.

3 Using a spatula, cover each cake thinly with the chocolate ganache.

4 On a surface dusted with confectioners' sugar, roll out the chocolate fondant using the rolling pin and the guide sticks.

5 Cover each cake with the fondant as described on page 17 and trim off the excess with a kitchen knife.

6 Use the fondant smoothers to straighten the sides and the top of the cakes.

7 Mix the white rolled fondant with different colors as you require. Roll out each color until very thin and cut out different rings and circles using the biscuit cutters.

8 Arrange these on top of the cakes to make different designs, using a bit of royal icing to stick the fondant on the cake.

9 Outline a few rings with white royal icing.

10 Cut pieces of satin ribbon in colors that match the decoration and stick them around the bottom of each cake with little dabs of royal icing.

miniature wedding cakes

As a specialist in making wedding cakes, I have noticed right from my very first commissions that although brides these days are still looking for something traditional, more and more they want a cake with an unusual twist to it. As this idea provides both a cutting cake and individual cakes that can be used as favors at the same time, it is no surprise it has become one of my bestsellers. Another advantage of this cake is you can offer your guests a choice of different cake flavors.

It is best to make as much of this as possible in advance: try to start making the top tier and the miniature cakes 2 days ahead, the sugar flowers at least 1 day ahead, and the chocolate ganache half a day ahead.

FOR ABOUT 80 MINIATURE CAKES AND ONE 6-INCH TOP TIER

1 sheet of orange-flavored cake, 12 x 16 inches, using 1 recipe quantity basic sheet cake batter (see page 12)

1 sheet of lemon-flavored cake, 12 x 16 inches, using 1 recipe quantity basic sheet cake batter (see page 12)

6-inch round chocolate cake, using ½ recipe quantity basic sheet cake batter (see page 12)

¾ cup sugar syrup (see page 15) flavored with finely grated orange zest, orange juice, and Grand Marnier

⅓ cup orange marmalade

⅔ cup orange-flavored buttercream (see page 14)

¾ cup sugar syrup (see page 15) flavored with finely grated lemon zest, lemon juice, and Limoncello

⅓ cup lemon curd (I use best-quality store-bought)

⅔ cup lemon-flavored buttercream (see page 14)

½ cup plain sugar syrup (see page 15)

1 cup chocolate ganache (see page 15) flavored with peppermint liqueur

1 pound white marzipan

11 pounds white ready-to-use rolled fondant

⅓ cup apricot jam, strained

generous 1 cup royal icing (see page 24)

confectioners' sugar for dusting

80 5-petal flowers (see page 27) in 2 different shades of pink

green food color

EQUIPMENT

✳ large serrated knife

✳ pastry brush

✳ plastic wrap

✳ 6-inch round cake board

✳ round biscuit cutter, 2 inches in diameter

✳ 2 large trays

✳ large rolling pin

✳ ¼-inch guide sticks

✳ 18 yards satin ribbon, ¾ inch thick, in 2 shades of pink

✳ small saucepan

✳ kitchen knife

✳ fondant smoothers

✳ parchment or waxed paper

✳ paper pastry bag (see page 25)

✳ 4-tier cake stand (try to rent one from a local cakemaker)

✳ 25 bright pink fresh roses and 25 pale pink fresh roses, plus some extra petals, to decorate

TO FILL THE CAKES:

1 Once your cakes are cool, trim the top crust off each of them using a large serrated knife.

2 For the orange cakes, slice the sheet of orange cake in half and soak the tops of both layers with the orange-flavored sugar syrup.

3 Spread one layer with orange marmalade then with orange buttercream, and sandwich the other on top. Wrap in plastic wrap and chill for at least an hour until firm.

4 For the lemon cakes, slice the sheet of lemon cake in half and soak the tops of both layers with the lemon-flavored sugar syrup.

5 Spread one layer with lemon curd, then with lemon buttercream and sandwich the other on top. Wrap in plastic wrap and chill for at least an hour until firm.

6 For the 6-inch top tier, slice the round chocolate cake into 3 layers and soak each one with the plain sugar syrup.

7 Layer the cakes with the peppermint-flavored chocolate ganache. Chill for at least 1 hour until the ganache has set.

8 Once set, stick the chocolate cake onto a 6-inch round cake board with a dab of the ganache and coat it with ganache until even and smooth; chill again.

9 Take the chilled orange and lemon cakes out of the refrigerater and cut out circles from them using a 2-inch biscuit cutter. Each sheet should produce about 40. Place them on a tray, wrap in plastic and chill again until needed.

TO DECORATE THE CAKES:

10 For the top tier, remove the chocolate cake from the refrigerator. Cover the cake with the marzipan and then 18 ounces of the white rolled fondant as described on page 17; let everything set for 1 day.

11 Once set, lay some dark-pink satin ribbon around the side and fix in place with a dot of royal icing.

12 For the miniature cakes, bring the apricot jam to a boil in a small pan. Remove the little cakes from the refrigerater and brush the tops and the sides with the jam, using a pastry brush.

13 On a surface dusted with confectioners' sugar, roll out some of the white fondant, using ¼-inch guide sticks.

14 Cover each cake with the rolled fondant and trim off excess. Use fondant smoothers to smooth the top and the sides. Place the cakes on a tray lined with parchment or waxed paper and let set overnight.

15 Once set, attach a small piece of satin ribbon around the bottom of each cake with a dab of royal icing. Use one shade for each flavor, so you will be able to differentiate the cake types when serving them.

16 Stick a 5-petal flower in a shade matching that of the ribbon on top of each cake with a dab of icing.

17 Mix a little bit of royal icing with some green food color, snip the tip of a paper pastry bag in a "V" shape and pipe small leaves around each flower.

ARRANGING THE CAKES:

18 Place the 6-inch cake on the top tier of a cake stand. Arrange the little cakes on the tiers below, leaving some gaps for fresh roses.

19 Arrange fresh roses and petals all over the cake stand and the top tier.

chocolate canapés

I wanted to create a smart, cosmopolitan cake design that could be served as both a sweet canapé at cocktail parties and a *petit four* after dinner. I think these little stripy squares fit the bill. They are totally stylish and look best when on a simple plate. I like to think Paul Smith might offer these at one of his fashion shows. Serve them on the day they are made.

MAKES ABOUT 120 SQUARES
(about 60 of each color combination)

1 sheet of cake, 12 x 16 inches, using
   1 recipe quantity basic sheet cake
   batter, flavored and soaked to your
   choice (see pages 12–13)
¾ cup plain sugar syrup (see page 15)
⅔ cup chocolate ganache (see page 15),
   flavored with peppermint liqueur
14 ounces white ready-to-use rolled
   fondant
food colors (yellow, orange, blue)
7 ounces chocolate-flavored
   ready-to-use rolled fondant
confectioners' sugar for dusting

EQUIPMENT
* plastic wrap
* large spatula
* small rolling pin
* kitchen knife
* small plastic board

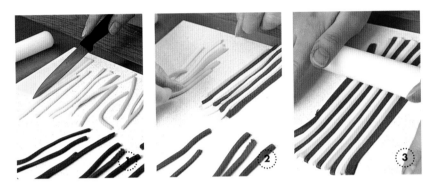

1 Wrap the soaked cake in plastic wrap and chill for 2 hours until firm.

2 Once firm, spread the cake with a thin layer of chocolate ganache, using a large spatula.

3 Divide the white rolled fondant into 4 equal parts and color them in yellow, orange, blue, and green. (Use a mixture of yellow and blue to achieve this last color.)

4 Roll out the chocolate fondant to ¼ inch thick and cut into thin strips about ⅛ inch wide. Repeat with colored fondant (see 1).

5 The color combinations shown are chocolate, orange, and yellow, and chocolate, green, and blue, but

it is up to you to decide how you would like to arrange colors. Choose 2 different color combinations. Cut the cake sheet in half and cover each half with a different color. Do one at a time by arranging the stripes in alternating colors next to each other on a plastic board or surface dusted with confectioners' sugar (see 2). Use a rolling pin to roll them out very thinly so the fondant is large enough to cover half of the cake. By rolling them out close to each other, the strips will stick together (see 3).

6 Trim off the edges of the cake and the fondant so you end up with clean and straight sides.

7 Cut each sheet into 1-inch squares using a damp sharp knife.

stripy rose cakes

Smart stripes and candy pink are more fashionable than ever, and help turn these pretty pastries into couture cakes. I recently made these cakes for a friend and, for a change, decorated them with stripes in vivid rainbow colors—they were a great hit.

FOR ABOUT 15
BEGIN THESE AT LEAST A DAY IN ADVANCE

½ sheet of cake, 12 x 16 inches, using 1 recipe quantity basic sheet cake batter, flavored, soaked, and filled to your choice (see pages 12–15)

⅓ cup apricot jam, strained

confectioners' sugar for dusting

1½ pounds white ready-to-use rolled fondant

generous 1 cup royal icing (see page 24)

pink food color

15 pink sugar paste roses with green calyces (see page 28)

EQUIPMENT

✻ plastic wrap

✻ 2-inch round biscuit cutters

✻ small saucepan

✻ pastry brush

✻ small rolling pin

✻ ¼-inch guide sticks

✻ small kitchen knife

✻ 2 fondant smoothers

✻ parchment or waxed paper

✻ paper pastry bags (see page 25)

1 Wrap the soaked and filled cake in plastic wrap and chill for about 2 hours until firm.

2 Using a 2-inch round biscuit cutter, cut out about 15 circles.

3 Bring the apricot jam to a boil in a small pan and, using a pastry brush, brush each cake all over with the jam.

4 On a surface dusted with confectioners' sugar, roll out the rolled fondant to ¼ inch thick using guide sticks. Cover each cake with the fondant as described on page 17.

5 Trim off the excess fondant using a small kitchen knife.

6 Use the fondant smoothers to straighten the sides and top of the cakes. Place on a sheet of parchment or waxed paper and let dry for 1 day.

7 Once the fondant has set firm, fill 1 pastry bag with soft-peak icing in pastel pink and another with soft-peak icing in bright pink.

8 Pipe lines as shown, starting at the top in the middle, lifting the bag and bringing it slowly down to the bottom of the cake. Touch the end point and stop piping (see Basic Piping Techniques on page 25). Pipe one line next to the other in alternating colors, keeping the lines nice and straight.

9 Finish the lines by piping small dots in the same colors along the base.

10 Stick a rolled fondant rose on top of each cake with a dab of royal icing.

"stripes and candy pink are more fashionable than ever

fantasy cake slices

When I first came to London to begin studying pâtisserie, I quickly learned all about the delightful English tradition of afternoon tea. Although I loved the concept right from the start, I have always felt it needed some fresh ideas. These fantasy slices combine simple and yummy cakes with charming and playful designs that are guaranteed to be a success at your next tea party. The cakes are ideal for mixing and matching different flavors and colors, so feel free to experiment a little bit and create your own favorites.

There might seem an awful lot of steps to this, but it is one of those methods that looks much more complicated than it actually is—it is more or less the same procedure done three times with subtle differences.

FOR ABOUT 24 SLICES

1 sheet of vanilla cake, 12 x 16 inches, using 1 recipe quantity basic sheet cake batter (see page 12)

1 sheet of chocolate cake, 12 x 16 inches, using 1 recipe quantity basic sheet cake batter (see page 12)

1 sheet of pink cake, 12 x 16 inches, using 1 recipe quantity basic sheet cake batter (see page 12) just adding a drop of pink food color to the batter before baking

1½ cups sugar syrup (see page 15)

2 cups vanilla buttercream (see page 14)

18 ounces white ready-to-use rolled fondant

food colors (yellow, pink, and green)

confectioners' sugar for dusting

9 ounces chocolate-flavored ready-to-use rolled fondant

selection of 4 different sugar flowers, such as daffodils, 5-petal flowers, pansies, and daisies (see page 27, you will need 72 flowers, or 18 of each)

EQUIPMENT

* large serrated knife
* large plain knife
* pastry brush
* large spatula
* plastic wrap
* large rolling pin
* ¼-inch guide sticks
* 2 fondant smoothers
* paper pastry bags (see page 25)

1 Trim the crusts off your cakes using a large serrated knife.

2 Cut each cake into 4 equal rectangles (12 x 4 inches), so you have 4 white, 4 pink, and 4 brown rectangles of cake.

TO MAKE THE YELLOW CAKE:

1 You need 2 layers of pink cake and 1 of white. Starting with a pink layer, soak the top with sugar syrup and spread it with buttercream, using a large spatula.

2 Place the white layer on top, soak the top with sugar syrup, and spread it with buttercream as before.

3 Place the remaining pink layer on top and soak it with sugar syrup.

4 Now trim the long sides of the cake neatly, using a serrated knife.

5 Cover the whole cake with a coat of buttercream, but don't cover the ends. Chill for about 1 hour until the buttercream has set.

6 While that is chilling, mix the white rolled fondant with a little bit of yellow food color until pastel yellow. Keep it covered in plastic wrap until use.

7 Once the buttercream has set, roll out the rolled fondant on a surface dusted with confectioners' sugar using a rolling pin and ¼-inch guide sticks.

8 Apply a thin layer of buttercream on the top and sides of the cake as before to make the rolled fondant stick, and cover it with the fondant (see page 17).

9 Trim off the excess fondant with a small knife and smooth the top and the sides with the fondant smoothers.

10 Now cut off the ends of the cake with a sharp knife so you can see the beautiful layering of the different-colored cakes.

11 Slice the cake into 6 equal pieces, making sure you wipe the blade of the knife after each slice for a clean finish.

12 Now arrange 3 pink 5-petal flowers on top of each slice, sticking them in place with a dab of royal icing.

13 Finish the look by adding little green leaves and curls to the flowers, following the same techniques as for the Bollywood Heart Lollipops on page 35 and repeating the same design on each slice.

TO MAKE THE PINK CAKE:

1 You need 2 layers of white cake and 1 of pink. Start with a white layer, soak the top with sugar syrup and spread it with buttercream, using the spatula.

2 Place the pink layer on top, soak the top with sugar syrup, and spread with buttercream as before.

3 Place the remaining white layer on top and soak it with sugar syrup.

4 Now trim the long sides of the cake neatly, using a serrated knife.

5 Cover the whole cake with a coat of buttercream, but don't cover the ends. Chill for about 1 hour until the buttercream sets.

6 While that is chilling, mix the rolled fondant with a little bit of pink food color until pastel pink. Keep it covered in plastic wrap until use.

7 Coat the top and sides with a thin layer of buttercream, cover with the rolled fondant, trimming etc., as with the yellow cake until you have the 6 equal pieces.

8 Now arrange 3 pansies on top of each slice, sticking them in place with a dab of royal icing.

9 Finish the look by adding little green leaves and curls to the flowers in the same way, repeating the same design on each slice.

TO MAKE THE BROWN CAKE:
1 Using the 4 layers of chocolate cake and the remaining pink and white cake layers make 2 brown cakes. Starting with a chocolate layer, soak the top with sugar syrup and spread it with butter-cream, using the spatula.

2 Place a pink layer on top of one chocolate layer and the white one on the other. Soak the top with sugar syrup, and spread it with buttercream as before.

3 Place the remaining chocolate layers on top of each cake and soak them with sugar syrup.

4 Now trim the long sides of the cakes neatly, using a serrated knife.

5 Cover both cakes with a coat of buttercream, but don't cover the ends. Chill for about 1 hour until the buttercream has set.

6 Cover the cakes with rolled fondant (this time the chocolate-flavored fondant), trimming etc., as with the yellow and pink cakes until you have the 6 equal pieces from both brown cakes.

7 Now arrange 3 daffodils on top of each slice, sticking them in place with a dab of royal icing.

8 Finish the look by adding little green leaves and curls to the flowers in the same way, repeating the same design on each slice.

large cakes

Valentine's heart

It is easy to make a simple heart-shaped cake look very special. The romantic floral border cascading down the sides of the cake makes a striking frame for a personal message or someone's name on top, so it can be used as a billet-doux for any sort of romantic occasion. Begin this cake at least one day in advance.

FOR AN 8-INCH CAKE

(about 25 party portions)

1⅔ pounds pastel-pink ready-to-use rolled fondant

1¼ cups royal icing (see page 24)

2 8-inch round cakes, using 1 recipe quantity basic sheet cake batter, flavored to your choice (see page 12)

¾ cup sugar syrup (see page 15), flavored to your choice

generous 1 cup chosen filling (buttercream, see page 14, or chocolate ganache, see page 15)

confectioners' sugar for dusting

1⅓ pounds white marzipan

2 tablespoons clear alcohol, such as vodka

selection of food colors

EQUIPMENT

* 12-inch round or heart-shaped thick cake board
* pink satin ribbon, ⅓ inch thick
* flower nail
* parchment or waxed paper
* metal piping tips for flower-making (see page 26)
* paper pastry bags (see page 25)
* large serrated knife
* large metal spatula
* 8-inch heart-shaped cake board
* pastry brush
* rolling pin
* ¼-inch guide sticks
* kitchen knife
* 2 fondant smoothers
* tilting turntable

1 Cover the 12-inch thick cake board with 5 ounces of the pink rolled fondant and the ribbon, following the instructions on pages 17 and 18.

2 Meanwhile, using the flower nail lined with pieces of parchment or waxed paper, royal icing, and a selection of different piping tips, make a selection of sugar flowers, enough to cover the sides of your cake, as described on page 27. Leave to dry overnight.

3 Trim the top crust off both cakes using a serrated knife. Cut 2 heart shapes out of the cake using the 8-inch heart-shaped cake board as a template.

4 Soak and layer the 2 heart-shaped cakes with your chosen filling.

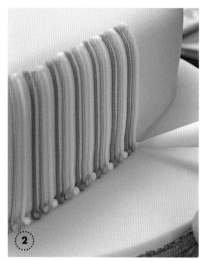

5 Coat the outside of the cake with the same filling and chill for at least 2 hours.

6 Once chilled, give the cake another coat of ganache or buttercream to make the marzipan stick to the cake.

7 On a surface dusted with confectioners' sugar, roll the marzipan out between ¼-inch guide sticks using a large rolling pin.

8 Using the rolling pin to help you, lay the marzipan over the top of the cake and push it down the side. Trim away the excess with a knife.

9 Use the fondant smoothers to make the top and sides nice and even; let set overnight.

10 Brush the outside of the marzipanned cake with a little bit of alcohol to make the rolled fondant stick to the marzipan.

11 Cover the cake with the rest of the fondant following the same technique as for the marzipan; leave everything to harden overnight.

12 Once hardened, pipe a dot of icing in the center of the prepared thick cake board and place the cake on top. Let it set for 1 hour to make sure the cake sticks firmly to the board.

13 Prepare 3 pastry bags filled with soft-peak royal icing in 3 different shades of pink.

14 Place the cake, on its board, on top of a tilting turntable. Tilt it slightly to the side away from you and then start piping lines down the sides, starting from the top edge down to the bottom edge and alternating the 3 shades. (See 1 and Basic Piping Techniques on page 25.)

15 Pipe a border of matching dots along the bottom of the cake (see 2).

16 Arrange the sugar flowers along the top edge to form a frame around the heart shape, using royal icing to stick the flowers in place (see 3).

17 Fill another pastry bag with green stiff-peak royal icing and pipe a couple of green leaves between the flowers, as described on page 35.

three-column wedding cake

This is a rather unconventional version of a classic wedding cake, in that the different tiers are placed next to each other instead of being stacked on top of one another. The elegant dot design is very easy to accomplish and gives this cake its romantic charm. Decorating cakes with fresh flowers has become very popular and the beautiful cascading roses adorning my cake here were kindly arranged by one of London's top floral designers, Rob Van Helden, whose glamorous creations are second to none. Your florist should be able to supply the oasis dome shape holders. Alternatively, just ask them to arrange the flowers for you. Make sure the roses have not been treated with any chemicals because they come in contact with the cake. Begin this cake at least three days in advance.

FOR ABOUT 100 PORTIONS

8 pounds white ready-to-use
  rolled fondant
food colors (pink, orange, yellow)
6 sheets of cake, 12 x 16 inches,
  each using 1 recipe quantity
  basic sheet cake batter, flavored to
  your choice (see page 12)
2½ cups sugar syrup (see page 15),
  flavored to your choice
6¾ cups buttercream (see page 14) or
  other filling of your choice
confectioners' sugar for dusting
6⅔ pounds white marzipan
2¼ cups royal icing (see page 24)
a little clear alcohol, such as vodka

EQUIPMENT

* plastic wrap
* 20-inch thick round cake board
* about 2½ yards pastel-pink satin
  ribbon, ¾ inch wide
* large serrated knife
* 3 6-inch thick round cake
  boards
* small kitchen knife
* pastry brush
* small and large spatulas
* large rolling pin
* ¼-inch guide sticks
* 2 fondant smoothers
* paper pastry bags (see page 25)
* 3 small oasis dome flower holders
* 3 4-inch thin round cake boards
* scissors
* about 100 fresh roses in pastel
  yellow, peach, and pink

1 At least 2 days ahead, color your rolled fondant: mix about 4½ pounds with pink food color, 2¼ pounds with orange, and 1¼ pounds with yellow. Wrap separately in plastic wrap until use.

2 Use about 18 ounces of the pink fondant to cover a 20-inch cake board and then decorate the sides with pastel-pink satin ribbon as described on page 18; let dry for at least 2 days.

3 Also at least 2 days ahead, trim the top crust of each cake sheet using the serrated knife.

4 Using a 6-inch round cake board as a template, lay it on top of the cake sheet and cut three 6-inch circles out of each sheet. (You will need 18 such circles in total.)

5 You will need 1 tier consisting of 3 cake circles, 1 tier consisting of 6 cake circles and 1 tier consisting of 9 cake circles.

6 Using a pastry brush, soak the top of each tier with sugar syrup and, using a spatula, fill each tier with the filling of your choice as described on page 16. Place each tier on a 6-inch round cake board, fixing it in place with a dab of buttercream or chosen filling.

7 Cover all the cakes with marzipan as described on page 17 and leave to set for at least a day.

8 Next day, cover the cakes with rolled fondant as described on page 17. Use the yellow rolled fondant for the small tier, the orange rolled fondant for the middle tier, and the pink rolled fondant for the large tier. Leave to set for at least a day.

9 Once set, fill 3 paper pastry bags with soft-peak royal icing of the same color as the different fondant-covered tiers and pipe small dots evenly all over the cakes. Should any of your dots form a peak, push it down with a damp brush while the icing is still wet, as shown above. Finish the top edge with a piped border of royal icing as described on page 25. Leave the icing to dry for a couple of hours.

10 Pipe some royal icing on top of the large iced cake board to make the cakes stick to the board and position the 3 iced cakes as centrally as possible on top, using the large spatula.

11 Soak the oasis dome flower holders in water and place them on top of the cake with a thin 4-inch round cake board underneath to prevent the water from running onto the cake.

12 The flowers should stay fresh for up to 1 day, so if your wedding starts in the afternoon I recommend you arrange the flowers no earlier than the late morning of the event. Cut the stems of each rose down to about 2 inches from the head.

13 Stick the roses into the dome-shaped holders and lay some roses loosely on top of the cakes so they are cascading from the top tier over the middle tier down to the bottom tier. Scatter some rose petals randomly over the cake board.

14 Remember to make sure that the flowers are removed from the cakes before they are cut and eaten.

gift box cake

If you are invited to a birthday party and you don't really know what to take, this cake is the ideal solution. Not only does it look like a genuine gift box, but the shimmering satin-like bow combined with the playful pink polka-dot design turns this simple cake into a funky, appealing present for people of all types and all ages. Begin the bow at least three days ahead and the cake at least two days.

FOR AN 8-INCH SQUARE CAKE (ABOUT 36 PORTIONS)

3⅓ pounds white ready-to-use rolled fondant

food colors (mint-green and pink)

1 tablespoon Tylose Powder

aqua shimmer dust

2 tablespoons clear alcohol, such as vodka

2 8-inch square cakes, using 1 recipe quantity basic sheet cake batter, flavored to your choice (see page 12)

¾ cup sugar syrup (see page 15), flavored to your choice

generous 1 cup filling of your choice (buttercream, see page 14 or chocolate ganache, see page 15)

confectioners' sugar for dusting

1⅔ pounds white marzipan

small amount of stiff-peak royal icing (see page 24)

EQUIPMENT

✳ plastic wrap

✳ small rolling pin

✳ small plastic board

✳ small kitchen knife

✳ thick soft decorating brush

✳ tissue paper

✳ parchment or waxed paper

✳ 8-inch square cake board

✳ serrated knife

✳ pastry brush

✳ large spatula

✳ ¼-inch guide sticks

✳ large rolling pin

✳ 2 fondant smoothers

✳ selection of small round cutters in various sizes

✳ paper pastry bag (see page 25)

Start by making the loop for the sugar bow at least 3 days ahead.

1 Mix about 18 ounces of the white rolled fondant with a little bit of mint-green food color until the fondant is a light green color. Knead the Tylose Powder into the rolled fondant (it is a hardening agent and will make the fondant more flexible and stable), wrap it in plastic wrap and let it rest for about half an hour.

2 Once rested, take a piece of the fondant and feel how it has become a lot more flexible for molding and shaping. Using a small rolling pin, roll a piece of fondant out on a plastic board until very thin. Using a small sharp knife, cut a strip about 2 x 6 inches out of the fondant.

3 Remove the trimmings and dust the strip with the aqua dust powder, using a thick soft decorating brush (see 1 opposite).

4 Turn the strip upside-down (see 2). Roll some tissue paper into a cylinder about 2 inches in diameter, place it in the middle of the strip of fondant and wrap the fondant around it as shown (see 3). Pinch both ends together, using a little bit of water or alcohol to make them stick; transfer to a piece of parchment or waxed paper.

Repeat this procedure again for the other half of the bow. Let both dry for at least 3 days.

PREPARE THE CAKES:

5 Trim the top crust of both cakes, using the serrated knife. Soak them with sugar syrup and layer both with your chosen filling, as described on page 16.

6 Coat the outside of the cake with the same filling and chill for at least 2 hours.

7 Once chilled, take the cake out of the fridge, place it on top of an 8-inch cake board and give it another coat of ganache or butter-cream to make the marzipan stick to the cake.

8 On a surface dusted with confectioners' sugar, roll out the marzipan between ¼-inch guide sticks using a large rolling pin.

9 Lay the marzipan over the top of the cake and push down the sides. Trim away excess marzipan with a knife. Use the fondant smoothers to make the top and sides nice and even.

10 Brush the outside of the marzipanned cake with a little bit of alcohol to make the rolled fondant stick to the marzipan.

11 Cover the cake with 2 pounds of rolled fondant following the same technique as for the marizpan. Leave to set overnight.

DECORATE THE CAKE:

12 Roll out the leftover green rolled fondant for the bow and cut out 2 long strips of the same width as the bow and long enough to reach from one side of the cake to the other.

13 Dust each strip with the aqua dust powder as before (see 1). Using alcohol to stick the fondant to the

CREATING THE BOW AND DOTS

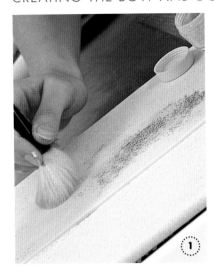

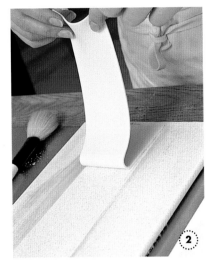

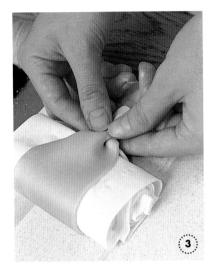

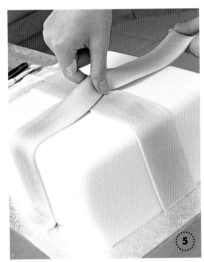

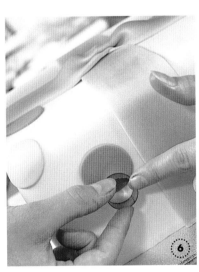

cake, lay the green rolled fondant strips across and over the cake. Pinch both strips together where they meet at the top of the cake (see 4 and 5). Trim the excess fondant at the sides using a small knife.

14 Color half of the remaining white rolled fondant pale pink and the other half bright pink.

15 Roll out the rolled fondant on a small plastic board and cut out circles in different sizes using round cutters.

16 Arrange these randomly on the white parts of the cake, using some clear alcohol or water to make them stick. Use small cutters to cut out a small part of large circles, then add small circles that will fit in the space (see 6).

17 Place the bow on top of the cake and fix it with a dab of royal icing.

18 For the end pieces of the bow, roll out another piece of rolled fondant as before and cut out 2 strips about 2 x 5 inches. Cut a "V" into one end of each and pinch the other ends together. Stick to the bow with royal icing and lay them on top of the cake in a wavy shape.

19 Finally, roll out another small piece of green fondant, dust with shimmer powder and wrap it around the middle of the bow.

pink wedding cake

This gorgeous and girly creation of pastel-pink icing and white hydrangea sugar blossoms will help give any wedding that "fairytale come true" feeling. Begin this cake at least three days in advance. For an even more magical effect, you can sprinkle the white blossoms with some white edible glitter while they are still wet.

FOR ABOUT 130 PORTIONS

11 pounds pastel-pink ready-to-use rolled fondant

2 6-inch round cakes, each using ½ recipe quantity sheet cake batter, flavored to your choice (see page 12)

2 8-inch round cakes, each using ⅔ recipe quantity sheet cake batter, flavored to your choice (see page 12)

2 10-inch round cakes, each using ¾ recipe quantity sheet cake batter, flavored to your choice (see page 12)

2 12-inch round cakes, each using 1 recipe quantity sheet cake batter, flavored to your choice (see page 12)

3½ cups sugar syrup (see page 15), flavored to your choice

4½ pounds (about 9 cups) buttercream (see page 14) or other filling of your choice

11 pounds marzipan

confectioners' sugar for dusting

2¼ pounds (about 4½ cups) royal icing (see page 24) for making the flowers

pink food color

EQUIPMENT

✳ 16-inch round cake board

✳ large serrated knife

✳ pastry brush

✳ large spatula

✳ about 5 yards white satin ribbon, ¾ inch wide

✳ 6-inch thin round cake board

✳ 8-inch thin round cake board

✳ 10-inch thin round cake board

✳ 12-inch thin round cake board

✳ large rolling pin

✳ ¼-inch guide sticks

✳ 2 fondant smoothers

✳ paper pastry bags (see page 25)

✳ piping tips (Wilton 103, PME, etc.)

✳ flower nail

✳ parchment or waxed paper

✳ turntable

✳ 12 plastic dowels

1 Cover a 16-inch cake board with 12 ounces of pink rolled fondant (see page 17). Cover the sides with white ribbon.

2 You'll need 4 cake tiers, each consisting of two 2-layer cakes (see opposite). Trim, soak, and fill each tier as on page 16, then set on an appropriate thin cake board; chill.

3 Cover each tier with marzipan as on page 17; let set overnight.

4 Pipe the hydrangea blossoms in different sizes using stiff royal icing. Make as 5-petal flowers (see page 26), but only pipe 4 petals. Mix a little of the icing with pink food color and pipe the stamens in the centers; let dry overnight.

5 Next day, cover each cake with pink rolled fondant as on page 17. Let set for one more night.

6 Once set, assemble the tiers and the cake board on top of each other as described on page 19.

7 Arrange ribbon around the base of each tier. Stick flowers along the sides of each with stiff royal icing.

English rose wedding cake

I recently saw a wallpaper design by Cath Kidston in an interiors magazine that inspired this cake. I simply love the old-fashioned effect, it's so beautifully British and makes me think of English rose gardens. The technique used for painting the flowers on the cake is called "brush embroidery." If you haven't done this before, you might find it a bit difficult at the beginning, so I suggest you try it out on a cake board iced with rolled fondant first until you are happy with the results, before you start with the cake. Begin this cake at least three days in advance.

FOR ABOUT 110 PORTIONS

7¾ pounds white ready-to-use
   rolled fondant
food colors (pink, yellow, and green)
2 6-inch round cakes, each using
   ½ recipe quantity basic sheet
   cake batter, flavored to your choice
   (see page 12)
2 9-inch round cakes, each using
   ¾ recipe quantity basic sheet cake
   batter, flavored to your choice (see
   page 12)
2 12-inch round cakes, each using
   1 recipe quantity basic sheet cake
   batter, flavored to your choice (see
   page 12)
2½ cups sugar syrup (see page 15),
   flavored to your choice
3⅓ pounds (6¾ cups) buttercream (see
   page 14) or other filling of your choice
confectioners' sugar for dusting
6¾ pounds white marzipan
2¼ cups royal icing (see page 24)

EQUIPMENT

* about 1¾ yards bright pink satin
   ribbon, ⅛ inch wide
* about 1¾ yards bright pink satin
   ribbon, ¾ inch wide
* 1 16-inch thick round cake board
* 1 thin 6-inch round cake board
* 1 thin 9-inch round cake board
* 1 thin 12-inch round cake board
* large serrated knife
* pastry brush
* large spatula
* large rolling pin
* ¼-inch guide sticks
* 2 fondant smoothers
* rose and rose leaf embossers
* paper pastry bags (see page 25)
* fine decorator's brush
* turntable
* 2 thick 3-inch round cake boards
* 2 thick 6-inch round cake boards
* 2 thick 9-inch round cake boards
* needles
* 8 plastic dowels
* scissors

1 Mix about 12 ounces of white rolled fondant with pink food color until it has a deep fuchsia-pink color, similar to that of the ribbon you are using. Use this fondant to cover a 16-inch thick round cake board as described on page 18. Cover the sides of the board with the ¾-inch wide satin ribbon.

2 You will need 3 cake tiers, each consisting of two 2-layer cakes, one 6 inches round, one 9 inches round, and one 12 inches round. Trim, soak, and fill each tier as described on page 17, then set on an appropriate thin cake board.

3 Cover each cake with marzipan as described on page 18 and let it set overnight.

4 Before covering the cakes with rolled fondant, have rose and rose leaf embossers ready. Cover each cake with white rolled fondant, as described on page 17.

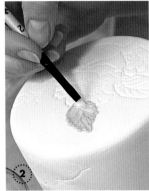

5 While the rolled fondant is still soft, push the embossers carefully into the fondant of each cake to create an all-over rose-and-leaf design (see 1). Leave to dry overnight.

6 Color your royal icing and prepare your pastry bags. You will need several pastry bags filled with soft-peak royal icing in each of the following colors: fuchsia pink, pastel pink, green, and yellow.

7 Start with the green leaves: pipe the outline of the leaf shape using the green icing. Take a fine decorating brush and dampen it with water. Use the brush to pull the icing from the outside into the middle of the leaf (see 2), which will create the veins of the leaves. Repeat for all the leaves, cleaning your brush from time to time.

8 When finished with the leaves, pipe the pink flowers: pipe each rose a petal at a time. Pipe one line of fuchsia-pink icing on the outline of a petal and pipe another line of pastel-pink icing next to it on the inside of the petal (see 3). Use

the damp decorating brush and pull the icing from the outside edge to the middle of the flowers so the 2 pink colors blend together. Repeat for all the rose petals, cleaning your brush from time to time.

9 To pipe the centers, take the yellow icing and pipe little dots into the middle of each open rose (see 4); let dry for an hour or two.

10 Place 1 tier at a time on a turntable and, using a pastry bag filled with white soft-peak royal icing, pipe a border along the bottom and top edge of each tier; let dry.

11 Stick two 3-inch thick round cake boards together with a dab of royal icing. Do the same with two 6-inch thick round cake boards and two 9-inch thick round cake boards. These will form the cake separators.

12 Cover the sides of each separator with the remaining wide satin ribbon and fix with a pin as on page 18.

13 Now assemble the whole cake. Mark 4 points in the middle of the bottom tier so they form a 5-inch square. Stick 4 plastic dowels into the cake at these points and cut them to the right length as described on page 19.

14 Repeat for the second tier, positioning the dowels in the middle to form a 2-inch square.

15 Stick the 9-inch round separator in the middle of the iced 16-inch thick round cake board, using a dab of royal icing. Center the 12-inch bottom tier on top.

16 Place the 6-inch round cake separator on the bottom tier so it covers the plastic dowels that are stuck inside the bottom tier.

17 Next, place the 9-inch middle tier on top, followed by the 3-inch round separator and finally the 6-inch top tier.

dropping daisies

Rather similar in concept to the earlier Pink Wedding Cake, this equally striking cake is made just that touch more playful by the addition of the white sugar bows and by the use of a refreshing mint green as the base color.

FOR ABOUT 90 PORTIONS

2¼ cups stiff-peak royal icing (see page 24)

yellow food color

confectioners' sugar for dusting

9 ounces white ready-to-use rolled fondant

small amount of clear alcohol, such as vodka, or water

filled and iced square two-tiered cake as described on pages 16–17

EQUIPMENT

* metal piping tip Wilton 104/103
* parchment or waxed paper
* flower nail
* paper pastry bags (see page 25)
* small rolling pin
* fine decorating brush
* small plastic board
* small kitchen knife

1 Using white and yellow stiff-peak royal icing, paper pastry bags, and piping tips, pipe 120 sugar daisies as described on page 27 in 3 different sizes; let dry overnight.

2 Meanwhile, on a work surface dusted with confectioners' sugar, roll the white rolled fondant out to a long strip and cut out two ¾-inch wide strips that are long enough to go around the sides of the cakes.

3 Brush the bottom edge of each tier with alcohol or water using a decorating brush, and stick the strips of fondant around each tier (see 1). Make sure you start and finish in the middle of the same side.

4 To make the bows, roll a smaller piece of fondant out on the small plastic board and cut out 2 strips ¾ inch wide and 5 inches long.

5 Using a small kitchen knife, cut 2 "V" shapes out of the middle of each strip opposite each other.

6 Brush the middle of each strip with a little bit of water or alcohol and bring both ends of each strip to the middle to form the bow (see 2).

7 Roll another small amount of rolled fondant out and cut out 2 pieces of about ½ x ¾ inch. Brush the middle of each bow with some water or alcohol and push 1 small piece of the cut-out fondant into the middle of each bow (see 3).

8 Stick each bow on to the sides of each tier where the ends of the rolled fondant strips join together, fixing them in place with some water or alcohol. Open up the bows' loops slightly to give them shape.

9 Finally, stick the daisies randomly along the top edge of each tier, using dabs of royal icing.

romantic rose tower

Voluptuous roses in luscious pinks and gorgeous butterflies "fluttering" at the end of curled wires turn this cake into a piece of pure romance. Inspired by *A Midsummer Night's Dream*, I designed this cake to create something different and unusual as a glamorous centerpiece for wedding receptions and birthday parties. It is very time-consuming to make, but is well worth the effort. You can make the roses a few weeks in advance, as they will keep well.

FOR ABOUT 120 PARTY PORTIONS

You need to begin this at least 3 days ahead and make your marzipan roses and leaves at least 24 hours in advance to guarantee they dry.

4 sheets of chocolate cake (see page 12)

1 recipe quantity chocolate ganache
(see page 15)

confectioners' sugar for dusting

4½ pounds marzipan

4½ pounds pink rolled fondant

a little clear alcohol, such as vodka

about 120 marzipan roses (see page 29) in different shades of pink

about 24 marzipan rose leaves
(see page 28–9)

pink royal icing (see page 24)

EQUIPMENT

* about 10 round templates with diameters from 2 to 12 inches for cutting out the cake layers
* 12-inch round cake board
* large spatula
* large rolling pin
* ¼-inch guide sticks
* small kitchen knife
* pastry brush
* paper pastry bag (see page 25)
* 16- + 18-inch round double cake boards covered with pale pink rolled fondant and deep pink ribbon (see page 18)
* wired feather butterflies (see Suppliers, page 143)

1 Using your templates, cut out circles of cake with diameters graduated from 2 inches to 12 inches.

2 Using a large spatula, spread a small amount of ganache on a 12-inch cake board and place the 12-inch cake on top. Spread a thin layer of ganache over this first layer and place the next-largest cake on top. Continue to assemble the cake layer by layer in this way to form a cone shape.

"this cake is pure romance"

3 Cover the whole cake with chocolate ganache and smooth the surface. Place the cake in the refrigerator and leave it to set for at least 2 hours.

4 Dust your working surface with confectioners' sugar and roll out the marzipan to a thickness of ¼ inch, using your guide sticks. Make a paper template that will be big enough to form a cone, when rolled, that will cover the cake. Use this to mark and cut out a triangle of marzipan large enough to cover the cake.

5 Once chilled, apply another thin coat of ganache to the cake.

6 Use your rolling pin to lift the marzipan triangle and carefully wrap it around the cake. Trim off excess at the top and the bottom. Leave it to harden overnight.

7 Next day, following the same procedure as with the marzipan, cover the cake with pink rolled fondant, but instead of using chocolate ganache to stick it on, first brush the cake with the alcohol. Let the fondant harden overnight.

8 Next day, pipe a dot of icing in the middle of the double cake board and place the cake on top.

9 Decorate the cake by sticking the marzipan roses and leaves on it with pink royal icing, starting at the bottom and working your way upward (see 1 and 2 above).

10 Finally, stick the wired butterflies into the marzipan roses evenly over the cake, using larger butterflies at the bottom and smaller ones at the top.

11 When serving, make everyone aware that the wired butterflies are not edible, and make sure they are removed before the cutting and eating of the cake.

templates ℓℓ

For reasons of space I haven't tried to supply templates for every project. You should usually be able to find appropriate cutters or make your own templates if you need to. Here, though, are templates for the two projects where they are really necessary (you have to pipe directly onto a template)—the Christmas Trees on pages 72–3 and the Butterfly Fancies on pages 76–9.

glossary

Most items listed here are available from specialist suppliers (opposite), although some of the more everyday ones can be found in supermarkets and bakeware stores.

Ingredients

DRIED EGG WHITE This powder is used instead of fresh egg whites in making royal icing for food safety reasons, as the dried egg white is pasteurized.

DUST, EDIBLE This nontoxic pearl dust comes in different shades. Edible dust can either be mixed to a thick paste with a drop of alcohol or it can be applied directly with a soft decorating brush. Also called shimmer dust.

FONDANT Made from sugar, water, and cream of tartar, fondant is widely used as a glaze in confectionery as well as in pâtisserie and cake decorating. Ready-made fondant is available from specialist suppliers or from supermarkets as a powder to be mixed with water.

FOOD COLORS The food colors used in this book are those in either liquid or paste form. The pastes are more concentrated than the liquids and, therefore, more useful for coloring rolled fondant and marzipans. Liquid colors mix faster and give more even results with royal icing.

GLITTER, EDIBLE Edible glitter is nontoxic.

GLUCOSE This is a thick version of corn syrup used to make fondant icing to give it a beautiful shine.

MARZIPAN Made from ground almonds and confectioners' sugar, marzipan is mainly used for covering large cakes before icing or frosting them, as it seals in moisture as well as helping to stabilize shape. Also, marzipan is ideal for making marzipan flowers (see pages 28–9), as it is very easy to mold and the individual petals stick to each other naturally.

ROLLED FONDANT A very smooth and pliable icing made from gelatin, confectioners' sugar and water, which dries hard. Rolled fondant is used for covering cakes and for making flowers and modeling cake decorations.

ROYAL ICING This decorative icing, made of sugar and egg white, or dried egg white, dries very hard and white, and can be easily tinted with food coloring.

TYLOSE POWDER If mixed into rolled fondant, marzipan, or royal icing, this harmless chemical, carboxymethycellulose (CMC), forms a strong modeling paste that dries hard. Tylose powder can also be mixed with a bit of water to make a thick and strong edible glue.

Equipment

BONE TOOL A long plastic stick with two rounded ends that looks almost like a bone, a bone tool is used for shaping the petals of rolled-fondant flowers.

CEL STICK This is a thin plastic stick for shaping flowers.

DOWELS, PLASTIC These long sturdy plastic sticks, which can be cut to the required size, are used to support the top tiers in large cakes.

FOAM PAD A foam pad is used as a yielding surface for thinning the edges of fondant flowers with a bone tool (see above).

FONDANT SMOOTHERS For icing cakes, you always need at least two of these. Fondant smoothers are flat rectangular pieces of smooth plastic, with a handle, that are used to smooth the marzipan and rolled-fondant icing on a cake.

FLOWER CUTTERS Made of metal or plastic, flower cutters are used to cut petals and leaves out of rolled fondant. In this book I have used cutters to make fondant pansies, daisies, and mini blossoms.

FLOWER NAIL A stainless steel flower nail is used for making royal icing sugar flowers. It functions as a convenient supporting base for the piping of daisies, pansies, daffodils, etc., since it may be turned readily in the non-piping hand.

GUIDE STICKS These long plastic sticks are used to roll out dough or rolled fondant to an even thickness, usually ¼ inch.

LEAF VEINER/VEINING MAT A rubber mat used for shaping and marking leaves made of rolled fondant or marzipan.

PIPING TIPS Stainless steel piping tips are used for piping flowers and leaves from royal icing. They are available in different shapes and sizes. My favorite brands are Wilton and PME.

ROSE AND LEAF EMBOSSER Usually made of plastic, embossers are used to push the impression of a pattern into icing. In this book I have used rose and leaf embossers to create the design for my English Rose Wedding Cake (see page 130–3), which I afterward painted over with a technique called brush embroidery.

ROSE CALYX CUTTER Metal or plastic cutters used for cutting a rose calyx out of rolled fondant or marzipan.

ROSE PUSH-IN MOLD A flexible rubber mold for shaping roses out of rolled fondant that is easy to use by simply pushing the fondant into the mold. The fondant rose is then released by turning the mold inside out.

SIDE SCRAPER Best made of stainless steel, a side scraper is a flat piece of metal with a straight side that is used for scraping the excess cream off the side of a cake when filling it. It will help give perfectly straight sides to your cake.

SPATULA A broad-bladed, long, flat knife without a sharp edge for use in spreading cream and other fillings. The angled spatula has an angled blade that makes it useful for lifting large cakes.

suppliers ϵϵϵ

For general cake decorating tools and equipment:

CopperGifts.com
900 N. 32nd Street
Parsons, KS 67357
www.coppergifts.com

Kitchen Collectables, Inc.
8901 J Street
Suite 2
Omaha, NE 68127
www.kitchengifts.com

New York Cake Supplies
56 West 22nd Street
New York, NY 10010
www.nycake.com

Sugarcraft, Inc.
2715 Dixie Highway
Hamilton, OH 45015
www.sugarcraft.com

Sur La Table
5701 6th Avenue South
Suite 486
Seattle, WA 98168
(With branches across the
United States.)
www.surlatable.com

Sweet Celebrations
1-800-328-6722
www.sweetc.com

Williams-Sonoma
Mail Order Department
PO Box 7456
San Francisco, CA 94120
(With branches across the
United States.)
www.williams-sonoma.com

Wilton
2240 West 75th Street
Woodridge, IL 60517
www.wilton.com

acknowledgments ϵϵϵ

Although I've been lucky enough to be making cakes for a lot of high-profile clients right from the start, I have always considered myself as quite a freshman in the cake decorating business. Writing a book has always been one of my goals for later, but I'd have never thought that this dream would come true so soon. I would like especially to thank Katrin Cargill, who got the ball rolling. She found me at a Christmas fair in Chelsea last year and introduced me to Jane O'Shea and Helen Lewis from Quadrille.

Jane and Helen, I would like to thank you both for giving me this amazing opportunity and for providing such an enjoyable and inspirational working atmosphere. I was given the most fantastic team of very inspiring people to create this book. I would like to thank my photographer, the gorgeous Georgia Glynn Smith for taking the most beautiful images of my cakes. I think you've brought the best out of them. Thank you Chalkley Calderwood Pratt for designing this book. I love your style and I think you're fabulous.

Writing this book has proven to be a lot more difficult for me than making the cakes and cookies. This is where I would like to thank my editor Lewis Esson, for giving me a lot of advice and for adding charm and flair to this book.

Last but not least, I would like to say my biggest thank you to my wonderful partner, Bryn, who has been my rock throughout this whole project. Without your devotion, none of this would have been possible.